INTERNET MARKETING

Photo of author on back cover by Mike Roberts (01639 820840)

INTERNET
MARKETING

HOW TO GET A WEBSITE
THAT WORKS FOR YOUR
BUSINESS

Nigel T. Packer

RIGHT WAY

Constable & Robinson Ltd
3 The Lanchesters
162 Fulham Palace Road
London W6 9ER
www.right-way.co.uk
www.constablerobinson.com

This edition published by Right Way, an imprint of
Constable & Robinson, 2008

While every effort has been made to ensure the accuracy of
URLs and links to websites provided in this book for
reference and further information, it is inevitable that due to
the very nature of the internet, by the time you read this
some may have changed and may no longer be valid.

Google screen shots courtesy of Google.
Microsoft product screen shots reprinted with permission
from Microsoft Corporation.

A copy of the British Library Cataloguing in Publication Data
is available from the British Library

ISBN: 978-0-7160-3020-1
Printed and bound in the EU

1   3   5   7   9   10   8   6   4   2

ABOUT THE AUTHOR

Nigel T. Packer has 20 years' experience of marketing in the public sector, manufacturing and charitable organizations. In the past six years, with his internet marketing consultancy, Business for Business, he has delivered training, seminars and speeches to audiences in the UK, Europe and USA, and helped thousands of small and medium businesses in both the UK and Europe to develop their internet business strategy and growth programmes.

CONTENTS

FOREWORD

Every book I have read about the internet and business seems to say, "Speak to your marketing department and agree a budget with them," or words to that effect. Yet most businesses I encounter do not have a marketing department and often have a budget of zero! The second part has to change, of course, as you don't get anything for nothing.

I wrote this book because whenever I stand up and speak at a conference, the delegates always want more. More information, more detail, more questions answered. I realize that many of those who attend do not necessarily have the business budget to be able to pay my consultancy fees. So I felt it was important to be able to communicate directly to them in an affordable way.

It took a long time to start as I wanted to be sure that I was writing for the right people: the business owners, the managers, the start-up companies and those who work with them. I hope that it will be useful for web developers who may not have business experience, helping them to get a broader view of business and how the internet fits in to the commercial picture.

I was determined that it wouldn't be just another book in the long list of books about the internet. You know the ones – full of theory, situated between the get-rich-quick books, the ones with 'killer-website' in the title, the ones that are apparently written for dummies (I don't know anyone who fits that category) and the large and heavy corporate business manuals.

I hope I have succeeded. Please let me know.

ACKNOWLEDGEMENTS

I want to acknowledge here the people without whom this book could not have been written.

My wife Lorna for her contributions on website usability and for providing insights on what it is actually like to be a web designer – not forgetting her constant support and belief in me. Oh yes and for providing excellent food to keep me and my spirits up when the task seemed very big.

My editor Judith Mitchell and the team at Constable and Robinson whose patient guidance has been invaluable. I hope we have a long and happy relationship.

Lastly, all the businesses, business owners and entre-preneurs who – over the years – I have met and talked to, or helped and advised with consultancy or training. They, in turn, have provided me with irreplaceable insights to supplement my own experiences as a small business owner.

INTRODUCTION

For anyone who is in business or thinking of going into business, this is a book about websites and using the internet for business.

For anyone who is a web designer or developer or thinking of becoming one, this is a book about business and the internet.

It is estimated that there are over 4.5 million businesses in the UK. The vast majority – more than 99 per cent – are classed as small businesses.[1] This business category includes (but is not limited to) sole traders; those individuals who are working for themselves as an alternative to employment.

Every entrepreneur or business owner I have ever met has dreams about a successful business; and many of those hope that they can make money online. "Everyone else seems to be doing it, so why not me?"

Sadly, expectations and reality do not always meet. I have spent many years providing business support as a consultant, as a business adviser and through the delivery of business training

---

1. In the UK in 2006 almost all business enterprises (99.3 per cent) were small (0 to 49 employees). Only 27,000 (0.6 per cent) were medium-sized (50 to 249 employees) and 6,000 (0.1 per cent) were large (250 or more employees). From the UK National Statistics Office at: http://stats.berr.gov.uk/ed/sme/smestats2006-ukspr.pdf.

and seminars. Through these activities I have come into contact with many website owners who express disappointment and frustration about the lack of results their businesses seem to achieve through the internet.

Over the years I have built up a picture of the problems that they all share. While everyone's story is different, some universal themes and experiences emerge.

One of the most common reasons for failure is a lack of the business owner, director or manager, taking control of, or fully engaging with, the website development project. I don't mean that they should do it themselves; on the contrary, I rarely recommend this course of action. Rather, that management by abdication rarely works in any part of a business. This understandably results from fear of technology, confusion over jargon and the enormous amount of information that is out there, that, by the time you have learned it, has already changed.

Another common phenomenon is the breakdown in communication between the business and the web designers or developers. To be more accurate, it is more often that the business and the web designers do not even seem to speak the same language, let alone be on the same page. This can mean that they fail to communicate effectively at all. Hardly surprising when the majority of businesses do not seem to understand how their website should be helping their business, and many (though, of course, not all) web designers and developers have little or no knowledge or experience of business.

Often disguised as a problem with the website, or about the internet, there are often more fundamental problems with the business. The most common of these is a lack of detailed understanding of who their customers are, how they behave, what they need, and why they buy (or don't buy).

New websites continue to be published every day, most of which are poorly designed and do not function well or to the benefit of the customer or business. These business websites consequently frustrate the customers, driving them away with a simple click on the back button in the browser.

Business and website owners and managers need to be working towards the removal of barriers to the customer, and to accept that they must be in control of their website projects.

Whatever business you are in, I am sure that, like me, you have a passion for your industry or subject. The skills and knowledge you have built up over the years mean that, just like me, every time you encounter something relevant to your profession which is not quite right, it jars you and makes you shudder.

Over the years I have reviewed thousands of websites in the course of my professional activities. I interrogate the sites relating to how they are performing in search engines but, more importantly, how they are performing for their users – the businesses' customers.

Like most people these days, I use the internet for leisure, for knowledge and research, and of course to purchase goods and services. Unlike most people, however, each time I look at a website I often find it difficult to stop myself slipping into professional mode – especially when it comes to something that could be easily corrected, but that is preventing the website from making a useful contribution to the firm's business strategy.

Back in the late 1990s when I was developing a strategy for an online business, it was hard to find information on what I needed to know and what would bring me the best for my new business in this virtual world. What was available was often highly abstract, written by academics and theorists. This made very interesting reading, but not what I was looking for. It didn't help me take my business plans forward in any way.

I found a complete lack of anything really aimed at the small or medium-sized business. Many mighty volumes existed aimed at the corporate manager; the big businesses with their marketing departments filled with bright young things who had degrees in every conceivable marketing subject. All seemed focused on those large international conglomerates that have vast budgets for the research and promotion of their business activities.

Despite much effort I found nothing that could really help or guide me, the entrepreneur.

This led me to develop the skills of the internet marketer and, a decade later, I have helped countless businesses to benefit from the opportunities that the internet offers.

If you have a small or medium business (no matter what sector), or are considering embarking on a business enterprise, then this book is for you.

It is a guide through the maze of getting a website that works for your business; showing how to take a common-sense, straightforward approach and harness the power of the internet; how to take control of your project by understanding what is involved and, through this, benefit your business.

By going back to basic business and website principles, this book walks you through the process of organizing the development of an effective website for your business, chapter by chapter. Wherever possible I avoid jargon and explain or analogize principles in everyday or business terms.

Through real-life experiences, leading to some thought-provoking observations, I have set out realistic ground rules to work to. By the end of the book you should be better prepared to work with your web designers or developers, and to understand and define the parameters that you want for your business website. I have tried to paint pictures that we can all understand and keep you, the reader, focused on who your website is for: your customers.

This is the one thing on which we should all be crystal clear if we are in business: without customers we have no trade and without trade there is no business.

1

WHAT IS WRONG WITH THE CURRENT WEBSITE?

If you buy a new household appliance or have something electrical or electronic fitted in your home or office, I wonder exactly how long you spend reading the instruction manual that usually accompanies it. Whether it is a folded sheet of A4 or some mighty tome of information, very few of us ever give it more than a cursory glance before diving in and having a go.

Of course, it might just be a new kettle; surely a kettle is like any other kettle? You fill it with water, plug it in and then it switches itself off; maybe it whistles to let you know that there is boiling water for tea or whatever. We all know how to use a kettle; this is partly because the basic design of a kettle has not changed in hundreds of years and an electric kettle has not changed much since it was invented in 1922[1], the water goes in there and this bit plugs in and here is the switch to press and off we go.

Muddling through?

We also take this attitude to things we are not so familiar with. We try things out and often succeed – to a point – by just

---

1. Arthur Leslie Large invented the electric kettle in 1922.

muddling through. No matter that we might miss features or perhaps not be aware of an easier way, we just carry on. All this time we are forming some mental model of how things work and often explaining to ourselves why something happened that we didn't expect, usually blaming ourselves for any mistakes or malfunction.

If something is too complicated, most people will just abandon it. Either they reject it completely – by using it less often because it is just too much trouble – or, more likely, they ignore the complicated features (often missing out the best bits) and just use the basic functions. For example, I have a juicer that makes fantastic healthy juice from whole fruit and vegetables. It's a great pick-me-up first thing in the morning, helps with the five-a-day thing and I get all my vitamins and so on. However, it takes ten minutes to dismantle the juicer to clean it and I just don't have the time.

Hands up if you have ever successfully programmed your video or DVD recorder for a TV programme that was on when you were away on holiday or business. If it worked, are you sure it wasn't a fluke (or involved a pre-teenager)?

In life we function perfectly well without ever really under-standing what is actually going on around us or how things work. For example, over 70 per cent of adults in the UK hold a valid driving licence;[2] it is logical to assume that most of them probably drive a car at some point. How many of those do you think could explain the principles and processes of an internal combustion engine, unless of course they were a car mechanic or maybe a *Top Gear* addict? Come to think of it, how many car mechanics could provide anything more than a basic explanation? I know car mechanics all over the country will hate me for this but in my experience the knowledge of a car mechanic mostly consists of: this bit needs to be tightly attached to that bit and, if this happens, then you need to turn

2. According to the Department for Transport's (at www.dft.gov.uk) most recently available figure (for 2005) 72 per cent of all adults aged 17 to 70 or over hold a current valid driving licence.

this bit until the light goes on, and so on. They are also just muddling through but with a little (or in some cases a lot) more knowledge and experience of cars than everyone else.

It's the same online, hardly anyone knows how the web works; or cares for that matter. Over the last ten years, in our consultancy and training activities, we have observed literally thousands of people using the internet and making the same mistakes over and over again. However clear the explanation may be, it often makes no difference; they just can't shift that mental model they have created – largely because there is no need to. It is astonishing to observe actions that so many think are the 'right ways' of doing something or the reactions of others who think it is their fault if something doesn't work as they expect.

The classic example of this is the vast number of people I have seen who habitually type the web address, complete with www.whateverwebsitetheyarelookingfor.co.uk into the search box of Google or some other search engine like Yahoo. (See Fig. 1.)

Fig. 1 How some people search for websites.

This is not because they have been taught to do it and have certainly never read it in a set of instructions, but because they think that *this is how the internet works*. Google or Yahoo or whatever has become their home page either by default or accident and so it is always their starting point.

I talk to people all the time who think that Google, Yahoo or most commonly AOL *is* the internet. These are not uneducated or stupid people; they commonly have higher degrees or hold down important jobs or run successful businesses, and often have been using the web for years.

Conventions

In reality, people learn to use things by experience in their day-to-day lives and not usually from books or training courses. If you use a specific thing often enough, it becomes normal – conventional. This doesn't mean it is the best way or the right way, it becomes the most common way and providers as well as users adopt these conventions because people are familiar with them and therefore know how to use them.

Take cars, for example. In virtually every car the accelerator is on the right, so it is a convention. If you were to design a car with the accelerator in a different place[3] it would be hard for people to learn or adapt to. It would be likely to inhibit the adoption of the design and therefore sales, so no-one does it.

The same thing applies to websites. In order to ensure that people have the best possible chance of finding your website easy to use, and therefore using it, then you must – as much as possible – stick to conventions. It is no surprise that the great website usability guru Jakob Neilson points out that since people use other websites more than yours (as there are millions of them out there), this means that they learn what is 'normal' from other websites not from your website.[4] In order to get the best possible results from a website we need to stick

---

3. The positioning of pedals in a car is such a critical problem, it appears that ½" too little space between them can make a car virtually undriveable. See discussion on this at http://forums.swedespeed.com/zerothread?id=37624.
4. **Jakob's Law of the Web User Experience**: users spend most of their time on *other* sites, so that's where they form their expectations for how the internet works. Jakob Neilsen's Alertbox column on website usability is free to access and a great source of straightforward information http://www.useit.com/alertbox/991003.html.

to the conventions that have developed and have been adopted as normal over the last few years, even if we think we can do better.

It has never been a good idea to try to reinvent the wheel. However, during the relatively short history of the web, this is exactly what has happened again and again. The internet is littered with websites that are virtually impossible to use or find. Interestingly, they often contain the same features and items that users dislike the most.

You may be one of the unfortunate or misguided who were unlucky enough to invest in something that seemed like a good idea or was the latest thing at the time, only to find you are now in possession of a big fat white elephant.

So how do you go about identifying if you are in this position with your website?

It can be a hard pill to swallow, but it is statistically likely that the website that you currently have is not providing the outcomes that you expected when you commissioned and published it a few years ago (or even this year for that matter).

In particular, if you went down the economy route and commissioned a website solely because it was the cheapest option or developed it yourself using a tool or template you bought online for $35, there is a high probability that it is not really suitable as a promotional tool for your business or as beneficial as you might like to think it is.

So why did you get the website in the first place?
We often ask our clients why they got a website, or what prompted them to go down that road at that time. While the answers vary a great deal some common themes constantly emerge:

- "The competition has one so we should get one…"

- "Let's get a website . . . I hear that companies are making a fortune online . . ."

- "The web developer told us that... looking back he was a really good salesman . . ."

- "Business advisers or Government representatives have all said that if you don't have a website you soon won't have a business . . ."

None of these reasons is sufficient or solid enough to have commissioned a website.

What you should have been asking yourself – before the site was developed – was: "Would a website benefit our business and how can we develop one that will strategically support or contribute to the growth or success of our business?"

What should I be asking myself now?
Now you need to be asking pertinent questions, among them:

- What does the website do for my business?

- Can my website be found by our existing or potential customers?

- Do we have any method of identifying this?

- Has our business changed focus or direction? If so, have we updated our website to reflect this?

- Is our website easy to use and does it serve some purpose or offer some service to our customers?

Your website is like a living, growing organism that needs to be kept alive by constantly updating and reviewing how it serves your business. If you do not feed it – with the changes that are taking place in your business – then it will stagnate and die.

If your website was not promoted online or offline when it was first published, or if there was promotion that hasn't been ongoing, it is unlikely that it can be found by your customers. Furthermore, is it constantly evaluated and adjusted to adapt to trends, so that it continues to be found and provide value to your business? It is possible that it may have been very good for your business in the early days when there was less online competition, but now through lack of attention you may be receiving less traffic, fewer enquiries or orders.

Think back to when your website was developed and the process you went through with the web developer. What was your expectation of your website and what were the objectives you set for the site at the very beginning? It is possible (and was very common) that very little consideration was given to such boring things as objectives in the excitement of the prospect of your business being on the internet. Perhaps you designed it yourself, or someone in your IT department did it. Does your site include things that are different for the sake of it or to 'make it stand out'? Perhaps your designer proposed something innovative and you were 'wowed' by the suggestion. Possibly you insisted on something being included because you thought it was amazing or maybe it came to you in a dream? Did you see something on someone else's website that really impressed you and, even though you didn't really know what it was for, you thought it would be really cool to include something like it in yours? Hopefully you are getting the drift of where we are going with this.

You and the internet
While I do not expect any reader of this book to have any kind of technical knowledge or experience, I am making the assumption that you use the internet on a regular basis, probably for shopping, whether products or the occasional holiday; perhaps researching suppliers and competitors, and definitely for email and business contact. I also assume that you are familiar with carrying out searches using Google or some other search engine. Of course, this chapter assumes that

you already have a website that is not performing as you expect and you are planning to get it sorted out. If you do not currently have a website, it is still a good idea to read to the end of this chapter as there are lots of details here on things to avoid in the future.

Whilst using the internet – whether browsing or searching – you are sure to have come across a number of common elements, features on websites, or other issues, that irritate, get in the way or just annoy you. So what is it about websites that you do not like?

This is a question that I have asked thousands of business people (and probably some of your potential customers) at the seminars and training workshops we have run through the business over the last ten years, while providing business consultancy or advice; when networking for business and even socially. Interestingly, many of the responses are the same regardless of where or of whom the question is asked; even more interesting (for me, anyway) is that the answers haven't changed much over the years.

What do people hate about websites?
The predominant reasons for disliking a website (not in any specific order) are:

- Welcome or splash pages.

- Flash websites. (These are websites that are constructed using the software Flash, not flashy websites though people hate those as well.)

- Big pictures with no purpose.

- Missing or difficult-to-find contact details.

- Websites that are difficult to navigate.

- Too little information/information overload.

- Pop-up windows.

- Small or illegible text.

- Letterbox sites.

- No prices.

There are obviously other things that people find irritating, but these represent the most common.

Welcome or splash pages

Welcome or splash pages (see Fig. 2) were very popular for a few years. In fact, many consultants and designers not only recommended them but practically considered it to be impolite not to say, "Welcome to our website", or words to that effect.

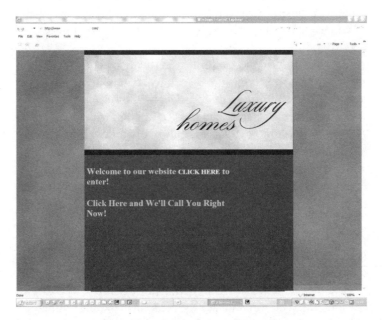

Fig. 2 An unnecessary welcome page.

Whilst you are interested in welcoming your customers you are also wasting their time. They want to get down to the business of searching or browsing or shopping, but your website is forcing them to take another stage or step before this can happen. The "Welcome to our website" or "Please feel free to look around the site and contact us if you want any further information" or even more irritating "Click here to enter" just represents a waste of the limited time anyone is willing to spend on your website. These days it is more likely to make someone click the back button as click to enter.

Flash introductions and websites
Flash websites are often characterized by their exciting appearance and are therefore appealing at first glance. The whole website can be a graphic wonderland of moving images or items that respond to your mouse movements (often with no real purpose). Huge on 'wow' factor, but not so good when it comes to taking into account the users' experience and needs.

Very difficult for the search engines to register and list in their results, Flash sites are usually seen by search engines' spiders and robots (the programs that work behind the scenes to register the site with the search engines) as a single image with no further information available to allow them to categorize the site in their database. You have probably not noticed that Flash websites rarely appear in the top ten results of a search engine enquiry. Our research shows that very few manage to do so (which is probably why you haven't noticed).

Flash is an amazing piece of software and used appropriately can be an extremely effective visual communication tool, but it must be used to *enhance* the message not try to *be* the message.

In addition, most people are irritated by being forced to wait for something they did not ask to see. If flash or other animation is used in a website, it should always be by invitation; that is, the viewer has the choice to see it, it does not launch or play automatically.

The flash introduction (often seen on a splash or welcome page) is the metaphorical equivalent to the high street retailer putting his foot behind the door when a customer tries to enter the shop and forcing the customer to "Please wait a moment (just loading . . .)" and then making the customer watch the promotional video before entering. Can you imagine the reaction of the customer standing by the door (in the rain)? Do you think the customer will stay outside for that time? Would you? I certainly wouldn't and ALL of the people we surveyed agreed. If you have access to your website statistics, take a look to see how many people do not get further than this point. (More about website statistics later in Chapter 13, Testing Testing Testing.)

Many flash introductions are an animated logo of some kind: maybe a series of tumbling letters that come together to form the name of the company or the elements of the logo appearing and building until the logo is finally visible. The user is often invited to click on the logo to enter the site or, which is worse, the animation just finishes and the user is left wondering what to do. Usually for the viewer's convenience a 'skip intro' link is provided. Do you click on the 'skip intro' link? I do and almost everyone we surveyed also skipped the intro. The only exceptions were those who had either: never noticed the skip intro links, or didn't know what it meant or was for. I wonder what the average return on investment (ROI) on a flash intro animation is. After all, if those who know what it is, skip it and those who watch it only do so because they don't know how to skip it, it certainly raises the question: who is it for?

Big pictures with no purpose
This refers to the use of large pictures that take more than a few seconds to download. This is not so much of a problem as it used to be before broadband was common. Back in the past,

those not-so-distant days of dial-up internet access, slow connection speeds and 56k or even 28.8k modems, any kind of picture other than the smallest icon was a problem and the more there were, the bigger the problem.

By their nature, pictures and images require relatively large files in terms of their digital size (video and music even larger, as the amount of information to be stored increases). Everything that you view on a website has to be downloaded from the web server (where the website is hosted) to your computer. The speed of this is limited by a number of factors: your connection (be it broadband or otherwise); how busy the server is or its capacity; and the size and number of files that need to be downloaded. Anything that makes the viewers wait should be avoided as it gives them the chance to leave.

If you need to display images to illustrate products or similar, then of course you must include them, but display a small version on the page, clearly offering the users an opportunity to view a larger version. This way the website users make a choice to wait for the picture to download and their experience is improved. User behaviour research constantly demonstrates that internet users want and expect choice. If they don't get it, then they go elsewhere.

On the subject of offering a larger version of the picture, make sure it *is* a larger version, not the same size or a little bit bigger! It seems this irritates just as many people; no-one wants their time wasted. Make it around twice the size (or larger, but not bigger than the viewable screen), with detail or alternative viewpoint options for optimum results.

Missing or difficult to find contact details
Once the mainstay of business research, it is a sad reality that many business people today use those big yellow books (yellow pages) as a doorstop. If someone wants a product or service they type the name of the company into a search engine and look for the contact details on the company's

website. If the details are either not on the website, or if they are but are very difficult to find, then how do you think that customer can make contact?

Many websites offer polite enquiry forms, but the incidence of these being completed and returned is very low. Part of the reason for this is that experience tells internet users that they rarely receive a response and are therefore wasting their time.

My own experience supports this:

- I recently received an email response from a form I completed online eleven months ago. It had taken so long I had completely forgotten what my query was and had no way of finding out. So when I got the (automated) reply I phoned them and asked why they were contacting me. They apologized and said that they had been experiencing difficulty with their computers. This did not engender confidence in any way. Is this how they would treat me if I were to buy their services? It is no longer an issue as the need had already been resolved with one of their competitors.

- They are not alone in this behaviour; I was sent an email inviting me to complete an online form to book a test drive in a new car with a major dealership. As it happens I was in the market for a new car at the time so I completed the form. I have never received a response. Needless to say I bought a different car.

- I am also still waiting for a very large software supplier to reply to an enquiry form after three years. The form on their website said I would receive a response within 24 hours.

When reviewing websites for clients I always fill in forms to test what the responses are like. Sadly the above examples are all too common with companies of all sizes.

Due to growing fears of becoming a victim of identity theft or online fraud, internet users are increasingly reluctant to reveal their details or give away too much information. In these times of identity fraud and spam email, most people are unwilling to reveal any contact details until they have made a decision to buy. This presents a barrier to anyone completing an online form that requires more information than is necessary for the type of enquiry.

It is important to remove any barriers to your customers' trust. If there are no contact details, then doubt is raised as to whether you are a legitimate business.

On this subject it is important to note that since 1 January 2007 it has been a requirement for companies registered with Companies House to include their company registration number and details of their registered address on their website.[5] Obviously, there are other legal requirements for websites but specifically what is required depends on what the website does or offers. If in doubt, always take qualified and specialist legal advice.

Websites that are difficult to navigate

There is no point in having lots of information on your website if your users simply can't find their way around it. If they can't find what they are looking for, they can't buy it.

Like all good things, the easier and simpler it is to use, the better the user experience will be. The design of the navigation system, particularly for large websites, is a crucially important factor of success.

The most common action on the internet is clicking the back button. When people who use your site get lost, they are more likely to click on the back button or leave your site than try to figure out where they are. The next usual action is to move on to the next site in the results page of the search engine to find whatever they are looking for in the hope that

---

5. For further details on this see: *Changes to business stationery rules* on the Companies House website at http://www.companies-house.gov.uk/promotional/busStationery.shtml.

it will be easier. This will be one of your online competitors. Furthermore, someone who has problems navigating your site is unlikely to return in the future for a second try.

Too little information

I have recently experienced this when trying to find the membership fee of an organization that I wanted to join. There were no fee lists on the site and no telephone contact numbers. It was too troublesome to try to find this information from other sources so I abandoned the quest. How many other people would like to join the organization but are put off by this simple need to know what the price of membership is?

Another common situation is lots of words and waffle but no real information. As discussed in Chapter 12, The Language of the Customer, people go to websites to find out information, and expect to find it easily.

If you were a potential client on your website and you couldn't find the information you were looking for, what would you do? Keep trying? Look for the contact details and telephone? This might be so, but maybe you just want to carry out research and don't want to speak to anyone at this point. Whichever way, not providing sufficient information is one of the most common barriers to sales.

Information overload

This is the opposite of the last item: websites that are stuffed full of poorly structured text and images, with links that don't make sense, compounded by multiple choices and lots of things in bold or highlighted, or popping up all over the screen to try to attract your attention. It is common to see websites full of marketing messages and calls to action but providing no real substance or information. Confused websites also fall into this category; those that are trying to do everything, where it is not really clear what each site is. Is it a shop? An advertising billboard? A club or a place to discuss topical issues? If you don't know where to start, as you are bombarded with mixed messages and multiple choices, then the resulting information overload is enough to make anyone leave and look elsewhere.

Pop-up windows
These are small extra windows that open either uninvited or when you move to a particular part of the website. They often contain adverts or sometimes special offers or surveys. See Fig. 3.

Less common than they used to be, there are still enough of them to irritate most users. Modern browsers such as Internet Explorer and Firefox now include blocking software to prevent pop-up windows opening automatically. This is now

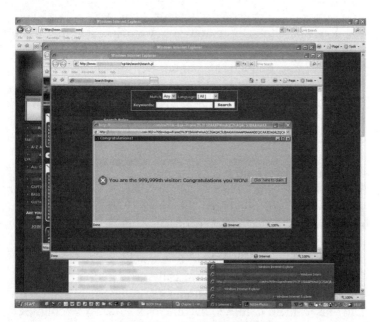

Fig. 3 Those irritating pop-ups.

usually a default setting, as there is a perceived risk of embedded viruses and other malware corrupting the computer. (Malware is a general term for any software that is meant to enter or damage a computer without consent. A virus is a type of malware.) So since the majority of users hate them, and most new browsers don't allow them, don't use them!

Small or illegible text

Web design, like graphic design, has trends and followers of fashion. A new trend in recent years has been the use of small text. Websites that have tiny unreadable text, especially when coupled with the inability to make the text larger (the option to do this using the browser settings should always be available) not only irritates many users but it is tiring and difficult to read. Not to mention the fact that it contravenes the guideline for accessibility compliance and the Disability Discrimination Act.

Coloured text on a coloured background has also become popular of late, one of the most popular being dark grey text on a light grey or tinted grey background. Again there are problems with accessibility as sufficient text contrast is essential for anyone with a visual impairment or even someone who needs glasses.

Choosing a font or typeface that does not display well on the screen, has poor readability or whose choice is downright bizarre is another cause of complaints. It is estimated that it is twice as hard to read text on a screen as it is to read from the printed page. Why would you deliberately choose to make it harder?

Letterbox sites

The way that a website displays on a given user's screen is dependent on a number of factors, one of which being the user's screen resolution. Resolution refers to the number of dots (pixels) that the screen is set to display. In addition, the way the website is set up and whether it is coded to display to a fixed width, or to adjust itself to the available width of the screen display, affects how the website looks.

A trend that has become more popular (or appears to be so due to higher screen resolutions) is the practice of designing 'letterbox' websites where the display is not just a fixed width but occupies a (sometimes small) rectangle in the middle of the screen. See Fig. 4.

The result is that the viewer has an experience which can be compared to trying to read a newspaper through a letterbox (hence letterbox websites). This type of website may be artistically pleasing or solve design problems but from a functionality perspective is a waste of money and a waste of space. Any impact that the visuals make is likely to be cancelled out by the restrictive nature of the website.

Fig. 4 A "letterbox" website.

No prices

What's that all about? Is the purpose of the site to tease people into seeing what you have but you are not going to tell them what you charge for the product or service? I am sure you have heard people say: "If you have to ask the price you probably can't afford it." This is a phenomenon common in the luxury goods markets: yachts, designer clothes, Rolex watches. Its use, therefore, implies to many viewers that it will be too expensive for them so the majority will be inclined to go elsewhere and find an alternative.

A few years ago I was called in to a small specialized retail business that used a website to promote their products. They had quite a good site, lots of relevant images and details, although no online transactions or credit card sales. Instead they encouraged people to phone them to place an order.

When I carried out a review of their competitors' websites, I noticed that none of them displayed their prices. One of my report recommendations emphasized the importance of including prices on the website to enable the visitor to make an informed decision. The owner's response to this was horror. "I can't put my prices on my website, as all my competitors will know what I am charging!" he exclaimed. I asked him if he knew what his competitors charged for the same products. He looked a bit sheepish and admitted that his secretary had phoned the competitors for prices pretending to be a customer. Had it occurred to him, I asked, that his competitors had done the same thing and as such they already know his prices? If so, he might as well put them on the website. He followed my advice (together with the other recommendations from the consultancy) and online business now contributes over 60 per cent of enquiries and subsequent sales. One benefit he had not anticipated was the reduced number of phone calls from people simply asking for prices who never made a purchase (some of whom were probably his competitors).

Other stuff

In addition to the above, there are a number of things that should be avoided and cause problems for your site in a way that the user may or may not be aware of. These include:

Frames

Frames are a method of setting up a website that involves splitting the page into two or more separate parts. Like partitions, the different sections contain different types of content and behave independently of each other. Commonly, one contains the navigation – the buttons and links to other pages – and the second contains the content. The content frame scrolls independently without the navigation frame moving. This method of design was prevalent in the late 1990s as it made it much easier to build a website. The web designer only had to create the navigation once and it could be automatically repeated on every page. However, there are various problems with a framed website, not least of all that its entire content looks like a single page to a search engine which reduces the effectiveness of the site as a promotional medium.

General overuse of technology for no apparent purpose

Adverts that flash or move in front of the bit you are reading (in an apparently telepathic way), bouncing balls, things that follow your mouse cursor movements, and, in particular, music that plays automatically when a website or a page is loaded (lots of people out there shopping online at their desks during work breaks – or otherwise) are all things that people say they hate and are enough to make them go to another site. Other things include the use of acrobat (pdf) files or anything that makes another application or program launch without warning.

All of the above relates to the user experience of those who actually find your website. By avoiding the things that everyone hates, the likelihood is that you will get more business as a result. If you have doubts about whether your website is easy to use or provides your potential customers with their desired results, then the only real way to find out is to test your website with real users. This needn't be as expensive as you might think; there are details on conducting simple user testing in Chapter 13, Testing Testing Testing.

Findability

What about finding the website in the first place? How can you tell if your website ranks highly in the search engines and can be found by those seeking your products or services?

Was there any marketing – online or offline – carried out, any promotion of the site, does it appear in the top ten places of a search engine results page for the important key phrases for your products and services that are pertinent to your business today? Can it be found easily? If the answer is no, then this is a major problem that needs to be resolved. If no-one can find you, then how can they buy anything from you?

The simple answer is to go through the process of carrying out sample searches yourself. This is quite straightforward, though very time consuming. Enter the keywords and phrases that represent your business products and services into search engines and identify where your website appears in the listings. This allows you to observe if the website is doing well. It also allows you to see where you are in relation to your competitors, and serves as a benchmark to record your progress when you make changes to your website.

Carrying out a full test on your site for all the keywords and phrases that are relevant to your products and services can take weeks if you perform a thorough survey. To reduce this time it is worth remembering that you only need to look through the first three pages of search engine results, as very few people look beyond page one of the search results with as little as 2 per cent reaching page three.

Website statistics

If you have access to your website statistics (there's some discussion on website statistics in Chapter 13, Testing Testing Testing) and have decided to get your website sorted out, now is a good time to 'benchmark' the site. This is a process that records the status of the site as it is now before you make any changes. This means that you will be able to observe the effect the changes have on the website and your business.

The kind of things you need to be looking at include: how many visitors are you currently getting to your website? How long do they stay, how many pages do they visit during a session, what keywords and phrases did they use to find your site and where did they come from to reach your site? These changing trends should be observed in order to gain some feedback as to what happens on your website and how your visitors behave, just like you might have management statistics or accounts that tell you the value of the average sale or how many people came through the door of your shop compared to how many made a purchase.

If you do not have access to this data, ask your web developer or website hosting company if it is available.

Accessibility

One of the biggest problems that is seen again and again as we review websites on behalf of our clients is the whole issue of accessibility. Put simply, if a website is accessible, then it can be used by the widest possible range of users – regardless of physical or mental impairment – all of which, of course, represent potential customers. In the UK, the Disability Discrimination Act 1995 includes websites (Part III Access to Goods and Services, and Part IV Education). A set of standards and Code of Practice have been established. On 1 October 2004, every website was required to meet the minimum standard by making reasonable adjustments, so by now, all websites should comply with the law.

Accessibility is no longer a matter of whether or not you consider that people with disabilities fit into your target customer profile. The term 'People with Disabilities' covers a very broad range. It could be someone who is completely blind and uses a screen reader[6] or someone who is simply colour blind and has difficulty with certain colour combinations. In general, detailed motor skills (such as using a mouse to click on a tiny icon or button) start to become harder for people over 50, and there are a lot of people out there who cannot use a mouse at all.

At the time of writing, the majority of people involved with web design have some level of knowledge of accessibility and how it applies to websites. There are many out there who know a lot about it and quite a few specialists. A recent search on Google on 'website accessibility' returned over 17 million references. Some offered automated testing and software tools (many free of charge), others offered information, guidance and articles, the most definitive of which can be found on the W3C website[7] which contains straightforward explanations and detailed guidance. There are also many consultants, experts and companies offering accessibility services and reviews.

Many designers and developers – particularly when accessibility first reared its head with relation to web design – felt then and still consider that accommodating accessibility means that they have to compromise. This sometimes leads to them ignoring the problem or being reluctant to acknowledge that it is their responsibility. Funnily enough, compromise can be exactly what it does mean, but then this is not necessarily something that I would expect designers to have an issue with. Graphic and web design are not about artistic expression or creativity; they are about effective communication of information on behalf of the client. Of course, aesthetics are important

---

6. A screen reader is a software application that converts the text of the screen into speech for those who are visually impaired.

7. On the World Wide Web Consortium Web Accessibility website at http://www.w3.org/WAI/.

but, if designers want to express themselves creatively (and maybe yours did), it would be better for them to look for a new creative discipline and move out of web design.

So where do we go from here?

If you have carried out a simple review on your website based on the information above, it is likely that you may have identified a number of issues that need to be resolved. The main points to consider relate to the purpose and process with which it was developed. Was it to meet business objectives? Are they still the same? With regard to your customers, what are the keywords and phrases that they use? How will you find out?

Hopefully you now understand that an effective website is one that is easy for your customers to find and use and one that tries to meet your business objectives. The next few chapters will discuss objectives and customers in more detail, as well as include a crash course in getting your hands dirty with a little technical knowledge (but only a little).

2

SETTING OBJECTIVES
FOR YOUR WEBSITE

Imagine you had been invited to attend a conference in a city or country far from your home. You decide to go as it might benefit your business if you were to attend.

What would be your course of action? I would hope that you wouldn't just walk out the door, get on the bus or in your car and go. You would make some kind of preparation before leaving; whether it was minimal or fulsome, you would probably make a plan.

You would be likely first to check on the dates and times, the location and maybe some other details (for example, what you needed to take with you, if food was to be provided and so on). You would need to arrange travel, so you might conduct some research to find out what was the fastest, easiest or cheapest method according to your priorities. Assuming you were to fly to another country, you might go to a travel agent in the high street or more likely online and find out which airlines flew to your destination, where their points of departure were, what the fares were, whether there were any extras, such as taxes or similar. You would hopefully remember to check that your passport was still valid for the date of travel.

This is turning into a very long list – although maybe a visit to a conference in another country is a big deal if it is not something you do all the time.

I wonder if you consider a website for your business to be a big deal. Your website provides the world with a window through which to take a look at your business. It has become the first port of call for many potential customers. I would certainly say that it is – or should be considered to be – a big deal.

Yet many people contract web designers or developers with no idea who their website is for, what it is supposed to do, or in fact any idea what their business objectives for having a website might be.

What do you want?

The web developer/client first meeting is a crucial one, but I know of many cases where the client when asked for some information, has responded: "Well I just want a website." And when encouraged to provide some more detail to respond, "Well you are the web designers, you tell me." You may laugh at this, or possibly you may find it to be a strangely familiar memory. If you leave the entire decision-making process up to them, the chances of you ending up with something suitable that serves your business well are very slim. More on this subject in Chapter 8, Communicating with Your Web Designers or Developers.

In essence, the web designers can only successfully design something to a set of parameters, or objectives. Many people consider design to be about making things look nice. There are many definitions of what design is; the one that I consider to be the most accurate is 'problem solving'.

It doesn't matter what the design discipline is, a problem or objective is the starting point. For example: design a chair that is comfortable and can be manufactured for less than £20. In relation to web design the problem or objective is more likely to be: enable my business to sell my motor spares stock throughout the UK. Any objective will be limited by some kind of constraints or parameters: the chair must be made of material from a renewable source and, due to manual handling regulations and to keep down transport costs, must weigh less than 15kg; the website must be manageable inhouse and be online by the end of this year.

Everything you decide to do in your business should have a clear objective. When I decided to write this book, my objective was to share my knowledge and experiences with those businesses that have a website which does not produce the results expected when it was originally commissioned.

I analysed the areas where there was greatest need, focused on small and medium business owners, directors and managers, and set about creating the structure and content of each chapter. As I progressed further, I discovered that the book actually needed to meet two objectives: to help those who already had a website and to guide others who were in the process of getting a new or redeveloped website.

I regularly deliver presentations to schools and colleges across the country on what it is like to run your own business. Each time I ask the students individually what they intend to do for a career. The most common response is: "I don't know." They usually do not have an end goal and so do not have the ability to set an objective and develop a route plan to get to their destination. Whether it is a career, a journey or the direction of your business, if you do not know where you are going, then how do you know if you have arrived and how can you plan to reach your destination?

Website objectives need to be focused on meeting the needs of your target customer, whether they need to order food to be delivered to their homes, get technical information or instructions regarding a purchase they have already made or check if a particular hotel in the chain is available on a given date. Some websites are likely to be focused to a large degree on the corporate side of business, supporting departments, branches or franchisees on operations, training or recruitment issues, or providing information to investors or the press.

Web design, like many other types of design, is about creating something that is fit for purpose, that meets the objectives of the project, so, by definition, we must set clear achievable objectives.

When you get down to it, there are only two possible objectives for a website:

- To generate income (through direct or indirect sales such as advertising).

- To inform.

You might dispute this. There are numerous objections and suggestions that we encounter all the time. I often challenge delegates at seminars to name a website or type of website that does not fit into one of the above categories.

If you find a site that you think doesn't fit into either or both of these categories (as shown in Table 1), then please challenge me.[1]

Once we have gained this broad understanding, the next step is to have a picture of what is possible on the web. The detail of this changes constantly, but fundamentally the general categories of business website are:

- Brochure website.

- Information provision.

- Direct sales – E-commerce.

- Integration – CRM (customer relationship management), logistics, order processing, etc.

  These are most often seen in combination, with e-commerce websites sometimes including lots of backup information, especially when they are selling IT hardware

---

1. Please let me know via my website at:
www.businessforbusiness.co.uk/bookfeedback.

Social networking sites e.g. MySpace or Facebook	Their business objective is to generate income through advertising and sponsorship deals, or the objective of the owners is probably to generate a lot of income by selling the site to the highest bidder.
Gaming sites	From sites where people can subscribe (pay money) to take part in a game with others around the world, to ones which offer free downloadable games (which are to encourage traffic and therefore provide leverage for advertising sales or as a taster for better games).
Charity websites	Always to generate income directly through sales or donations; to encourage people to volunteer in money-raising activities or to provide services; to inform those who have made donations about what has been done with their money and to encourage more donation through this action; to inform by raising awareness of the cause.
Review websites where the users can contribute or read independent reviews of anything from gadgets to holidays	Generate revenue from advertising; will be aiming to sell website space or advertising based on the number of users.
Mapping websites e.g. Google Earth, Streetmap	Generate income through advertising based on the number of users.

Table 1

and software; information sites like local authority sometimes take debit and credit cards for council tax and similar payments.

Brochure website

This type of site is defined more by what it doesn't do than what it does. It is often the initial type of website that a business undertakes, and does not have any ecommerce or online trans-actions; its fundamental purpose is to market the business. It might include a variety of information such as details of products or services, why or when the company was formed, where the branches are and so on. It takes the place of a traditional printed brochure. The advantage of having a brochure website is that it is often cheaper in the long run as you avoid reprinting costs when details or information changes. It provides the first port of call for anyone who wants to know about or contact your business. This is the minimum that *any* business should now either have or be planning for (not having a website has recently made the top-ten reasons for a business failing).

Information provision

Information sites are sometimes thought of as being the general preserve of the public sector. These are the local, regional and national Government, the police, fire and health service websites that have a duty to convey information to the populous, to educate and inform.

The provision of support information to the business' prospective or existing clients is not a method of income generation, but adopting the web as a medium for this can both save costs and create added value with relatively little effort. There are many types of information provision from providing technical specifications and comparison systems to aid in sales, to providing downloadable or interactive instruction manuals for products.

Another application is for PR purposes. It may appear that a website is providing information, but it can be a carefully crafted acquisition or maintenance of market share strategy. By maintaining the brand name and values in the mind of the customer, the website helps with continued sales.

Direct sales

On a website that accommodates direct sales, the visitor to the site can make the purchase online, instantly securing the product or service. Payment is made through some kind of secure transaction whether it is by credit card, debit card or by using an online service such as PayPal.

There are only a few types of product that are truly immediate direct sales where the purchase can be delivered or collected immediately. These are digital products and include: software, games, information in the form of reports and similar, music and, to a lesser extent at the time of writing, films, etc. These products can be downloaded to the customer as soon as payment has been received. Insurance could also be considered immediate in cases where the website confirms your insured status.

Most direct sales websites that take online payment are partial delivery systems. Booking sites for hotels, travel, theatres and tickets, or other kinds of bookings, use a voucher system with response being immediate or sometimes by email. The customer notes the confirmation numbers or prints the confirmation (now sometimes even containing bar codes), and presents it at the point of delivery: the ticket office, the hotel reception or the airport check-in desk.

Most of the direct sales websites use the same business model as traditional catalogue-based mail order, the website taking the place of the catalogue. The company receives the payment from the customer, then delivers the product or service at a later stage.

Indirect sales

Indirect sales cover a range of areas that help to make sales at a future point in time. In other words, they generate leads for your business. The site is used to generate interest from potential purchasers so that they contact you to make the purchase.

The most common indirect sales income on websites is advertising. This is really big business; online advertising in the UK has surpassed the overall spend on radio advertising and is expected to overtake TV as the primary advertising medium by the end of the decade[2]. Advertising sales are mainly based on the amount of traffic or registered users that a website can prove. This is now valuable leverage for either obtaining customers or achieving a higher price for advertising space.

So it all comes down to the question: what do you want your website to achieve for your business? Once this is established, you can begin to work out what functionality the website will require in order to satisfy these objectives.

Lead generation and the acquisition of new customers are the overriding necessities of all business. Therefore lead generation and sales are likely to be the primary purpose for your website; anything else you include as an objective is supplementary such as after sales service or customer support.

The more time you spend on planning, the better your outcome is likely to be. By setting clear objectives for your website you provide the foundations on which to build the rest of the project.

---

2. As reported in the Times Online on 5/10/06 at http://business.timesonline.co.uk/tol/business/industry_sectors/media/article660590.ece.

3

WEBSITE TECHNOLOGIES – WHAT YOU NEED TO KNOW

There is no getting away from it, if you want to be in control of your website development project, then you must at least have a modicum of understanding of what is going on out there in the scary world of technology.

Fortunately, to use the analogy of cars and driving (again), I would agree that you do not need to know how a car works in order to drive it, but you do need to know *how* to drive it; that the steering wheel makes it turn, etc. We are talking about a level of knowledge similar to: the right-hand foot pedal is called the accelerator, and you press it to make the car go. A level of understanding that allows you to realize that when you press the accelerator, fuel enters the engine somehow; if you press it harder more fuel goes in quicker. This may not be accurate or fulsome, but is sufficient.

Reading through this chapter is recommended, it will also serve as a glossary or reference for times when you think your web developers must be from another planet, as you have absolutely no idea what they are talking about. (This seems to happen to everyone at some point in the process.)

In the context of this book it is not possible (or appropriate) to cover all the multitude of jargon that exists in the industry. Many resources exist online; a search on 'website jargon' should produce a variety of links to useful information if you are interested in further reading.

A **website** is a collection of **webpages** through which you navigate using **hyperlinks**. Just like the rooms in a house, the hyperlinks provide doors from room to room.

Hyperlinks can be **internal** (from page to page in your website), **external** and outgoing, where you provide a link to another website; or external and **incoming**, where another website links to yours.

Your website essentially consists of two things: the structure and the content. The hierarchical structure that most websites adopt is navigated by the user using a system of **hyperlinks**. One of the building blocks of the internet, hyperlinks are HTML code that enables you to link or jump to another website, page or element.

Each web page is a separate entity, and exists on the computer as a file; just like you might have Word documents, picture or music files on your computer. Images and other elements that are not text also exist as separate files. They are not actually on the web page; instructions (that are not seen by the user) tell the web browser where to look for the file containing the picture.

HTML and other coding languages are used to develop the website. HTML stands for Hypertext Mark up Language and is the basic building block of a website. Lots of other types of programming languages are used for specific purposes including: SHTML, XML, XHTML, Java, JavaScript, and other scripting languages as they are termed. SQL is a language used to create databases. You don't need to know what these mean, just that they exist.

The first part of the HTML is called the **head code** and if you look at the HTML you will see it enclosed by <head> and </head>. This part of the code is used by the browser, the search engines and potentially other software.

Before your website can be published online you need to organize a **domain name**. This is a term commonly used to describe a web address such as www.yourcompany.co.uk. More accurately, **domain** refers to the last part: .com, .org and .net. These are called 'top-level' domains and are not attached to any particular country. Country specific domains are also in common use such as .co.uk (a company in the UK), or .org.uk (not-for-profit or charity in the UK). These are the most common domains in use for business. Other domains are available such as .eu for the European Union. From time to time new domains are released.

Domain name registration is the process of buying (registering) the name. This can be carried out yourself online; there are many agents and facilities on websites to do this, or your web designers can do it for you. Take advice before jumping the gun and buying a domain name; they impact on search engine results among other things.

URL stands for Uniform Resource Locator. Fortunately, you do not need to know that, but it is the correct term for what is normally called the web address. The address bar in your browser is where the URL goes or can be seen. See Fig. 5.

Fig. 5 Address bar with URL.

You would normally expect your website to be created by a **web designer** or **web developer**. The terms 'designer' and 'developer' (and 'web design' or 'web development company') are commonly (including in this book) understood to mean the same thing and are used interchangeably.

More accurately, 'designer' or 'web designer' normally refers to a person who is mainly concerned with the visual aspect of how a website looks and interacts with, or is experienced by, the user; how it communicates the brand identity and so on. This is often termed the 'front-end' of the website.

'Developer' or 'web developer' usually refers to a person who is mainly focused on the technology, the programming, the functionality, how it works and so on, often termed the 'back-end' (see also 'back-end integration', page 58). Web companies would often have a team that would include both of these.

Your website will need to be **hosted** on a **web server**. The arrangement of this is often carried out by your web designers or development company. A web server is a computer that is permanently connected to the internet and leases space for website files to be stored on their computers; internet users access them by typing the URL of the website into their browser.

A company that provides a good hosting service would be likely to have many web servers: very high specification computers with great banks of storage, usually maintained 24 hours a day, 365 days a year by a team of experts. It is not usually a good idea to try to host your website inhouse or to set up a computer as a web server unless you have this level of facilities and capacity in your company.

Website statistics provide information about the usage of your website. They are normally arranged as part of the hosting package; you would ask your web developers or person arranging your hosting to ensure you have access to your **webstats**. They come in a variety of forms, from lists of data to graphs. Review of webstats is an important part of the internet marketing process. They allow you to see data and information on the visitors to your site. Details vary according to the package but might include: number and duration of visits; the referrers (the place where the visitor was browsing last, such as a search engine when they followed a link to your site); the country of origin and time of day.

Website content consists of text, images and other elements such as sound and video.

Text is exactly what it says: text. Humble words on the page. It is, however, more important than it seems as text is what search engines catalogue and perform searches on. The text content of your website contains the keywords and phrases that will get your website to the top of the search engine results. It is also where most of the information is contained. It is therefore one of the most important factors that determines the success of your website. Unfortunately, text is often neglected or treated as the last hurdle to be leapt as quickly as possible. 'Content is king' is a much used saying that has been around for more than a decade. Nonetheless, this still holds true.

Images are normally in one of two formats: **jpeg** (pronounced *jaypeg*) and **gif** (pronounced with the g as in good) are the two main types of file. There are others, but they are much less common. Jpeg (which is an acronym for joint photographics experts group – but you don't need to know that) are used for photographs and what are called contone (from continuous tone) images, those which have blended and shaded tones and colours. Gifs are made up of flat colours and hard edges so are commonly used for logos, graphic elements and also for animations when they are referred to as **animated gifs**.

Animation or moving images are extremely powerful when used appropriately. Animated gifs are one type of animation format suitable for websites. Flash is a software program that is often used to produce complex and detailed animations or even entire websites. Think carefully as to whether your website, or more importantly, your customers will benefit from the use of animation or video before commissioning what is bound to be expensive development.

Video and video streaming are becoming more common on the internet. The roll-out of broadband has enabled the use of video to become popular. The large file sizes required by video previously presented a barrier; most users would not wait for the files to download. All this has now changed and websites such as YouTube have revolutionized the way video is used online.

enquiries

Please enter your contact information and brief details of your enquiry.

We operate a strict privacy policy, your contact information will not be shared with any third party without your express permission.

title	○ Mr ○ Mrs ○ Ms ○ Miss ○ Dr
name	
position	
business or organisation	
address	
tel	
e-mail	
I am interested in	☐ internet marketing strategy ☐ website audit & optimisation ☐ search engine registration ☐ training ☐ seminars & public speaking
other	

Send Form   Reset

Fig. 6 A simple form.

Music downloads are often (in recent times) many users' first encounter with the internet as they access websites to purchase and download commercial music. At the other end of the scale, one of the most hated website elements is music that plays automatically (very embarrassing when you are shopping online in your office and the boss is walking past just as the music starts).

Forms, also called feedback forms, are where you can collect user information, feedback or enquiries through your website. They can be forwarded to you by email or collected from your website hosting service. See Fig. 6.

If you are going to have direct sales in your website you will need: a **shopping cart (or basket)** facility. This is just what it sounds like: a virtual version of the trolley or basket where you put your purchases before paying for them at the

checkout where the purchaser's details (name, delivery address and credit card information) are collected so that they can be processed to take the payment in an **online transaction**. The term **e-commerce** is also used to describe this part, although e-commerce actually refers to the whole process of the display and selection of goods or services, the shopping cart, checkout and transaction process.

In order to process online **credit or debit card payments**, you will need a third party company to process the actual transactions (often for a fixed fee and/or a percentage of the transaction value). Examples of companies (there are many of them) that do this include Worldpay[1] and Protx[2] (which is UK based). This can be arranged directly with the company, your web development company might already have this set up or it can be organized through some of the high street banks.

In order to ensure that the credit card details are kept safe, the part of the website that handles the transactions must be on a **secure server**. When you are using the internet, the terms SSL, the first part of the web address being htts:// instead of http:// or the padlock appearing on the screen indicate that the server is secure. (See Fig. 7.) Secure means (in a general sense) that it is protected behind layers of security and that the data is encrypted, so the website can be trusted by the user.

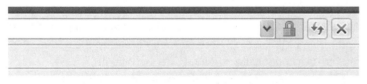

Fig. 7 A padlock symbol indicating a secure server.

Some websites choose to take payment by using an online service such as PayPal (now owned by Ebay) which allows payments to be arranged (for a fee) without the inherent

---

1. www.worldpay.com
2. www.protx.com

problems of setting up merchant accounts with banks, organizing shopping carts and secure servers.

If you have a large stock of products for sale or similar in your website, it will probably need to be **database** driven. A database is simply a large amount of information that is managed in a system. This is also a solution if you want to trade in multiple languages. Not all web designers produce database-driven websites. This is more the realm of programmers, so the company would need to have a team that includes database developers (software developers or programmers) to provide this.

Some websites require users to **login** or **register**. This is normally associated with a database of users (as opposed to products), where the user is required in the first instance to provide some details that will be included in the database. This would include a username and password (which might be allocated by the company as opposed to being chosen by the user). On subsequent visits they are then required to provide this username and password in order to access some, or all, of the website.

A **Content Management System** (CMS) is a piece of software that works alongside your website so that you can make changes to specific areas without any risk of inadvertently altering (breaking) your website. This would be set up by your web developers; you would need to purchase a licence for this extra software. If your website requires regular updating but is not really big enough to require the complexity and cost of a database, then a CMS is for you.

SEO or **Search Engine Optimization** is the process of selecting target keywords and phrases that reflect the content of the website or page and placing them appropriately in the website's meta names and content. It also includes the process of testing the search engine results, and making adjustments in response. It should be regarded as a continuous process although is more often treated as a one-off project.

Meta names are contained in the HTML code and provide

information about the webpage. They can have a number of different uses, and are often used to help search engines categorize the page appropriately. Even though they are contained in the HTML code of the webpage, they are in the head code section and are not directly visible to a user as the browser program does not display them. They can be seen by viewing the source code. A diagram of the head code can be seen in Chapter 5, Fig. 8.

Search Engine Registration is self explanatory and is the process of registering your website with search engines. With most search engines this now only has to be completed once for a given website, provided that appropriate code is contained in the website to instruct the search engine software to visit the site periodically keeping it updated in its records. **Spiders and robots** usually describe programs that search engines use to find out this information about your website. A spider is a type of robot, also called a webbot. You don't have them, the search engines do. What is important is that the spiders can access the information on your site.

Ranking refers to your website's 'importance' as far as a particular search engine is concerned. This is specific to an individual search engine and a given search term. In other words, your ranking for two different search *terms* will be different, and your ranking for the *same search term* in two different *search engines* may not be the same. It is your ranking that determines where your website appears in the search engine results page. Your ranking is affected by a number of factors including your search engine optimization and, in particular, the number and source of incoming hyper-links.

Online advertising can be in a number forms: **banner ads** or **tower ads**. Banners are wide and are most often seen at the top of the page; towers are tall and usually fit down the side of the page. These used to be very popular. However, research into online user behaviour has indicated that they are not as effective as once presumed.

Adwords are a Google facility. They are the adverts (that Google terms 'sponsored links') that appear on the top or the right hand side of the search results page. The website owner would **bid** for a specific keyword; the highest bidder for that keyword appears in the list at the top when that keyword is searched for. Adwords have been found to be one of the most effective forms of online advertising. Adwords are a type of **Pay Per Click (PPC)** advertising.

Affiliate or associate programs allow your website to advertise or promote items for sale that are being sold on another website. One of the websites that employs this to great effect is Amazon. You can post information on books and other goods (taken from their website) on your pages; when people click on the item in your website they are transferred to the correct page in the Amazon site; if they then purchase the item, you get a commission just like a salesperson.

Pop-ups and other irritating technologies are often used for advertising. If you are recommended them by your web designers or are tempted to use them, read Chapter 1 again.

If your website is large or you expect it to grow (in terms of number of pages), **search facilities** can be useful to the user. As a rule of thumb, if you have or are expecting in excess of one thousand pages (it is very easy to reach that), a search facility is essential.

Back-end integration – that sounds painful. And you probably can't afford it. More seriously, it is where a website is integrated in some way with the other technology systems in a business. For example, if someone buys an item from a website and it updates stock level systems, enabling automatic reordering. Or a purchase might update the accounting system enabling up-to-date management accounts to be produced automatically. If it works well, then it is fantastic, but this type of thing is still mainly the remit of large companies, as setting up and managing something like this is going to require a considerable investment of resources on an ongoing basis. As a rule of thumb, if you don't have an IT department (or at least an IT person), then you are unlikely to be doing this on any great level.

Other stuff you might have heard of or wondered if you need or want in your website includes:

Counters, also called hit counters, are small programs that count and display hits or sometimes the number of visitors on a website. These used to be very popular and almost every site you saw had one on the home page. Their presence can now mark your website as being old-fashioned or out of date in the eyes of most users. You don't want one on your site. If you want to know how many visitors or hits you are getting, you can look at your webstats. This is not information that you would want to broadcast to your users in any case – what if you have only had 51 visitors to your site? Ever. Not very confidence-inspiring if you have been online for a long time.

Uploading and downloading

When a computer sends data or information to another, it is called uploading. So when your website is published to the host server, it is uploaded to the server. When information is retrieved from another computer, the term is downloading. So you would download a web page to view it, or download a music file that you have purchased.

Downloadable files. Lots of files can be provided for download from a website, including files that you may be familiar with such as Word and Excel documents. One of the most common files to be made available for download from a website is an adobe acrobat file, also called a pdf (pronounced pee-dee-eff).

You may not have planned on learning any of this stuff, and the details above are certainly not on a technical level, but, sorry, you have to get your hands a little dirty in order to keep hold of your project.

**What you might think you need to know,
but probably don't**

Wikis are a common term for websites that are created collaboratively. They use a piece of software called a wiki which allows users who first have to register and then are able to create, link, edit and organize the content of the website. Wikis are usually information websites that contain reference material, reviews and recommendations or similar. Although not the first wiki (which was wikiwikiweb started in 1994), the best known at the time of writing is probably Wikipedia.

RSS or **RSS feed** is a type of web feed. This is a system used for providing users with frequently updated content such as news items or **blog** entries. Typically, the provider of the content offers some type of feed link on their website to which users of the website can register (for example, the BBC offers a 'news feed' on their website[3]). The users then access the information via a feed reader program (often occurring without any intervention from the user) on their own computer to view the content which is delivered automatically as it occurs or is updated by the provider.

Blogs or **blogging** has become commonplace today. The word is a contraction of 'web log' and originally described an online diary, although nowadays many consist of commentary or news on a particular subject. They are usually written and maintained by an individual (as opposed to a company). All sorts of people keep blogs, from teenagers on **social networking** websites to professional journalists and politicians. Often, though not always, blogging websites offer the facility for readers to post comments or responses, thus setting up a dialogue.

Online **social networking** is fast changing the way that society shares information and how individuals communicate with each other. Millions of people use social networking

---

3. At the time of writing, on the news page, at http://news.bbc.co.uk there is a link to 'news feeds' near the top of the page.

websites every day; for many it has become an integral part of everyday life. Perhaps the best known (at the time of writing) are MySpace, Facebook and BEBO. Many people will have encountered or heard of Friends Reunited, which was an early social networking website. The software used to create these websites allows communities to develop between people who share interests. The main types of services are based on categories or groups, and encourage connections and recommendations between friends.

Podcast refers to the distribution of digital media files over the internet that are available for playback on computers or some kind of portable media player. The term comes from 'iPod' (Apple's portable media player, which I have little doubt you will have heard of) and 'broadcast'. The term can refer to the content or the method of distribution.

Podcasters' websites often offer the ability to directly download their content, although a podcast is differentiated from other formats by the opportunity to be subscribed to and receive automatic notification when new content is added. Podcasts are often syndicated through **RSS** feeds, when they are termed podcasting.

The initial appeal was that individuals could distribute radio-type shows without the support of a large company or distribution network. Today it is used in a broad range of applications, including audio tours of museums and galleries. The education sector now makes very effective use of podcasting where distribution of lectures and lessons, discussions, assignments and other information is revolutionizing the education system.

4

WHO IS THE WEBSITE
FOR ANYWAY?

Many years ago I worked as a manager in an engineering company. As well as ensuring that the production floor ran smoothly, the role of business development became my responsibility, mostly due to the professional relationships I had established with the customers.

After a great deal of effort and preparation I managed to secure a large contract with one of our major customers. It was bigger than anything we had undertaken previously and had increased our company turnover by 300 per cent. Although the deadlines were tight, we were on schedule for planned deliveries and stood to make a large profit.

At the regular monthly management meeting, the company accountant thought it necessary to take me to task on the increased wages bill, in particular the amount of overtime payments. "If you weren't paying all this overtime," he said, "we could save the company a lot of money." My response, "If we weren't paying the overtime, then we wouldn't be getting the products to the customer on time and would lose the order," seemed to fall on deaf ears.

I have encountered this attitude again and again over the years. While I fully acknowledge that cash flow is often the bane of business and can often be a primary factor of failure in a small business, it is almost *never* a factor of success. You may have the most positive cash flow and the best planned finances, the most efficient operating systems, or even own patents for unique products. But there is no getting away from it – a business is nothing without customers, as I say in my seminars quite often: NO CUSTOMERS, NO BUSINESS.

Too many businesses simply do not place sufficient focus on or understand their customer and have no clear picture of who is the main customer for their products and services. If we take a look at any of the millions of websites online, it is not too hard to see that most of the sales messages, content and dialogue on these sites are not relevant to the needs of the users or potential customers of the company who owns the website.

It is not uncommon to see businesses that have simply taken their brochure and published it in digital form, converted, not interpreted or adapted to online conventions, instead sticking with the conventions of the print industry. They have not taken into account that people interact with the online world in a totally different way from physical printed media, brochures and promotional flyers.

Expectation among internet users of something better or at least different from a static page of print has increased as the internet has become mainstream. The conventions that are now taken as normal online do not require the user to be actually aware of this, for example: pages that link to each other, depth of information and the ability to experience the information in the order of the user's choice (as opposed to in a linear way – page one followed by page two and so on).

Many websites fail to satisfy their viewers, those customers or potential customers that seek the information, products and services offered. As I said above, one of the main reasons is that the owners or developers of those websites have insufficient knowledge of their customers. Fundamentally, if you do not understand or cannot identify who your main or target customers are, you are unlikely to be able to communicate to them in an effective way. The results of this can be mixed messages or confusion in your website visitors – customers.

It is not difficult to understand why this has arisen since the internet lurched unexpectedly into the commercial world. You may remember the publicity of the late 1990s by governments and advisers to get your business online. It was the same hype and excitement that pumped up the dot com bubble. Everyone thought that the internet was the new way to wealth and prosperity. It seemed that everywhere I went I spoke to someone, who knew someone, who was 'making a fortune' online. The message was clear: the paths of the internet were paved with gold, get a website or get left behind.

Almost a decade later, not having a website is often listed in the top ten reasons for business failure. However, having a website that is not focused on the objectives of the businesses, and more specifically the customers, is (like cashflow) unlikely to be a factor of success. In particular, I have noticed in the last few years a certain level of maturity developing in the way that some successful businesses use the internet. This has resulted in some key players surging forward and beginning to increase the competitive gap, leaving behind those who are not so enlightened.

Back in the 1990s, businesses everywhere rushed out and got anyone who could use a computer and had access to some software to build a website. Unfortunately, these were not always professionals (highly skilled designers or developers) but were more often the sons or next-door neighbours of the secretary or someone you met in the pub, who was 'brilliant with computers', even a 'whizz-kid' maybe and had built a website or two. They had little knowledge of, or concern for, the company they were working for and had even less under-standing of the company's customers. In addition, they were inexperienced in the world of business and had no concept of the principles of marketing and promotion.

Many of those who designed and developed websites in those early days had little knowledge of design principles (which, by definition, focus on the customer); instead much was simply 'made up' as they went along. In addition, of those who were skilled designers or interface developers, a culture of innovation was created to the point where many had such a free rein to do exactly what they pleased that elements that worked perfectly well and were understood by users were redesigned simply for the sake of it.

Often, when I have discussions or focus groups with web designers and developers I ask, "Why did you do this/change that/set it up in that particular way?" The answers are often, "Because I could/it seemed like a good idea at the time/to be different."

Some of the innovative things that were developed then have now become conventions and it is important to recognize this. Focus on the customer means that we must not only try to find out what customers want, what they are looking for, etc, but also how they are likely to do it, what it is they understand or find easy or obvious to use. Once something becomes a convention it is very hard to change as it becomes an expectation. This has nothing to do with the internet, it is human nature. That is not to say that the convention is the best or most efficient way of doing something.

Take for instance the keyboard that so many of us use every day to type our emails, reports and articles. Ever wondered why it is set up in the familiar but apparently illogical QWERTY arrangement? You might assume that it is something to do with the way letters are combined and actually is the fastest way to get something typed. No, it has been discovered that if you rearrange the keyboard layout, then its efficiency can be increased. In fact, it is a historical convention. It goes back to the invention of the mechanical typewriter. Due to the way the mechanism worked, if the typist worked too quickly then the levers carrying the type would jam. So the arrangement of the keys was changed, commonly used letters being placed far enough apart in order to *slow down* the typist.

When electronic typewriters and then computers were introduced, the first users were often secretaries or others who had learned to type on mechanical typewriters, so they expected the QWERTY keyboard. No-one wanted to re-learn how to type (it is considered by some to be as hard as learning a new language), also the cost of retraining was prohibitive.

Even though new faster keyboard layouts have developed and been brought to market, they have never caught on. This is no doubt because anyone who can already type sticks with the QWERTY layout, and those who have not yet learned to type usually find themselves faced with the prospect of being conventional. In addition, there is the risk factor: unless you are absolutely certain that you will only ever use your own keyboard, you will not be able to transfer your skill to the workplace, nearly everyone has QWERTY keyboards and therefore that is what you would expect to find.

The internet is changing how everyone carries out or thinks about making purchases, even the most mundane. Today, irrespective of our income, we have the option to go online and place an order for our groceries or other requirements. It is now so much easier to login to a store website during lunch break and have the whole list delivered during the evening. We might otherwise have needed to trail around a supermarket pushing a trolley, often with unhappy children in tow when we could have been doing something better. Home delivery usually within a few days is now normal and often free-of-charge.

The market leaders in the UK also have a fast growing business in many parts of the world. They spend millions of pounds a year analysing their customers' activities and the way their customers interact with the store via their loyalty/reward card system. This investment has helped them determine their business direction and the way they present themselves to those customers. Their promotional line for their online shopping service sums it up: 'You Shop – We Drop'. They treat their customers as the most important aspect of their business and their success is evidence of this.

Of course, in a small business we do not have the budget to carry out this level of customer research, but the realization of the real purpose of the store club or loyalty card (if it had not occurred to you before) can be enlightening. There are some basic activities that we can carry out in order to get a clear picture of our customers. In turn, this will help us produce the website that will help to improve our business, increasing our conversion of potential customers into revenue.

RESEARCHING THE CUSTOMER

You first need to make a clear definition of what type of market you operate in.

The first stage of this is straightforward. Are the products or services you offer aimed at:

- Other businesses – Business to Business (B2B)?

- The general public or end user of the product – Business to Consumer (B2C)?

- The third is not so often discussed – the Business to Public sector (B2P)?

If you are familiar with marketing principles, you will consider this to be obvious. However, the number of times I have asked the question, "Who is your customer?" and heard the reply "Everyone . . ." proves this is not an assumption that anyone should make.

So to deal with each in more detail:

Business to Business (B2B)

If the products or services you offer are for other businesses, you operate in a Business to Business (B2B) market. A common way to identify your clients or potential customers is by focusing on specific industry sectors, company size or geographical location that fall into your customer base. For example, if you are an accountant who provides limited company accounts, financial and management accounts, then you may be looking for businesses with more than ten employees who are listed on the Companies' House register, for companies in a specific area which is within a 25 mile radius of your location.

Business to Consumer market (B2C)

If you are selling to the domestic customer – i.e. you are operating in a Business to Consumer market (B2C) – your choice of criteria is much greater, but then so is the B2C market. There are lots of different things that can be measured: demographics such as age, gender, marital status, children, home ownership, income, occupation, lifestyle choices, etc. This is research that any business should be carrying out as a matter of course whether operating online or not. However, in practice I have found that this is seldom the case and most small businesses do not recognize the importance of such an activity. Getting a clear picture of what you are selling and who you are trying to sell to ensures that your marketing is effective.

Business to Public Sector (B2P)

One other sector is the Business to Public Sector or B2P. This can be identified from public information and includes schools, police forces, the fire service, local authorities and central government. This is much more easily defined and, if you work in a public sector environment, it is unlikely you will have difficulty with research.

THE RESEARCH

There are two forms of research: Primary and Secondary. I will deal with secondary research first:

Secondary research

Secondary research is information that *others* have already found out. This type of information is often available to the public, in the form of reports, statistics or documents. The results of the research will already have been analysed and structured in the form that was required by those who commissioned the research. The disadvantage of this is that it is often not exactly what you want to know, or may not apply to your business case specifically. The other issue is that, in order to verify that the research is valid and correct and has been interpreted in a way that you can trust, you really need to obtain the same information from a number of different sources.

Confused? What I am referring to here is the fact that you can't necessarily trust something just because it is written down or published. Newspapers make things up every day (the legal cases that are constantly in the news are evidence of this), events are reported from one person's point of view (as the old saying goes, the victor gets to write the history). If you use information that someone else has written, then in order to make sure it is true it is best to check out the information in a number of places. If they all say the same thing, then you can probably assume it is reliable. This is often not so easy.

A good place to start can be government websites such as the National Statistics Office[1], the Department for Business Enterprise and Regulatory Reform[2] and other departments that might be relevant to your business or industry.

---

1. www.statistics.gov.uk
2. www.berr.gov.uk

At the other end of the scale, research is carried out by specialist research companies and sold as reports. The reports they produce are often to enable decision makers to identify market trends and adjust their own business activities to meet variations in demand so they can maintain sustainability.

You can often glean some information from the executive summary of these reports, which are commonly available online free of charge to tempt the buyer to purchase the full report. Companies that produce this type of information have the reports available online and it is possible to purchase and download the reports directly from their websites. Examples are Keynote[3], Mintel[4] and RBA[5] where you can find links for many other research organizations covering hundreds of business sectors.

Primary research
This is information you find out for yourself, by interacting directly with the customer or potential customer. This is the really valuable stuff and, as you know the origin of the infor-mation, it does not need to be verified or checked out, and you have the opportunity to carry out any analysis and interpreta-tion yourself. However, if you are new to research, then it is not always easy to know where to go to obtain the information or to prepare, gather and analyse the data you collect.

How I approach primary research
I have always enjoyed fishing and during the summer holidays (the year I was aged twelve) I had great success one day selling my catch of mackerel door-to-door in the seaside village where I lived.

The following day I repeated the process but was surprised

3. www.keynote.co.uk
4. www.mintel.com
5. www.rba.co.uk

at the lack of sales; it seemed that no-one wanted to eat mackerel two days running and those who lived by the sea knew that they did not freeze so well. "Come back next week," was the answer from many. Making a mental note to do this, I took the fish back down to the beach to try to sell them. The beach was full of holidaymakers and day-trippers at that time of the year so there should have been plenty of potential customers. However, I could not understand why there were no takers. Everyone I asked, "Would you like to buy some fresh fish?" politely declined. I was a little dismayed but curious to find out why they were not interested, so I asked the next few people. The answer was quite consistent. As it was only mid-afternoon, they would be on the beach for a few more hours. If they purchased my fresh fish now the warm air and strong sun would soon dry it out and it would not be very nice to eat.

This I could understand so I went to the water's edge to rinse and refresh the fish with cold seawater. I repeated the process periodically and a few hours later – as the first people started to leave the beach – went around the crowds for a second time and sold them all.

The lesson here is that I had conducted (without realizing) my first primary customer research and it had paid off. I was in a position to have direct contact with my customers and had the nerve (or naiveté) to ask them why they weren't buying.

Carrying this out was fairly straightforward as I could speak directly to my potential customers. I was also in a position to have a quick response, making a quick decision on the course of action I needed to take. By altering my sales strategy I was able to ensure a good day's trade.

The owner of a shop or business where the customers call in regularly ('bricks and mortar businesses') have the advantage of potentially being in direct contact with customers and potential customers on a daily basis. Either in a formal way by conducting customer surveys or in a more natural way, during the course of conversation with customers, they are in a position to ask pertinent questions relevant to the business, their products and essentially the customers.

This is not so easily carried out for a business that trades only online via its website. By the nature of the internet, the customers could be anywhere from five to five thousand miles away, connected only by the website.

A common way to carry out primary research is to collect information through the website or by email in the form of surveys or questionnaires.

Considerable research has been carried out into the effectiveness of customer surveys, from face-to-face interviews to online collection. There are highly detailed analyses of the results of this research available online in a variety of places. In summary the data shows that the most effective type of survey is undoubtedly face to face. Response rates are between 40 and 80 per cent provided that the surveys are short (taking no more than five minutes to complete) and you explain why the survey is being carried out. Email and website surveys are not as successful in terms of respondents, and are becoming less so. A number of factors are responsible for this. Results have dropped since 2000 with an increasing wariness from participants and a resistance to spam and junk mail. Still, response rates vary between 2 and 30 per cent depending on the subject, the target age group and if there is an incentive. Even though response rates are lower online, it can be much more cost-effective to collect data online – once the forms are set up – as all the work is done by the respondent.

What questions should you ask?

As ever, you should set objectives first: why are you doing the research and what insights are you hoping to discover? From your objectives you need to develop a set of questions that will enable you to gain a greater understanding of what are the characteristics of the people who might purchase your products and services.

While it is not possible to define the exact questions that you need to ask for any specific industry, product or service in the scope of this book, the questions below should provide some guidance and focus to help you identify the sort of information that you should be looking for.

- Who currently buys our products and services?

- What type of people are they?

- Who are they buying from or how are these needs being satisfied now?

- Are the competitors selling to the micro, small, medium or large companies?

- Should we specialize in a particular sector (a set or type of customer or business which is buying similar goods or services, also called market segment)?

- Who else is selling into that chosen sector?

- What types of companies are buying in that sector?

- Who purchases the most in that sector?

In Table 2 we will take the training industry as an example and look at the approach that I took when I worked with a company setting up the training side of their business.

Identifying profitable customers
Where you start in this process depends on where you are in your business and how many or what products or services you are selling.

Assuming that you have been trading for some time, your sales records are invaluable for insights into performance and identifying the products that you are selling well; analysis of these is a good starting point. If your business has not begun trading yet, you will have to rely on forecasts.

Question	Answer
Who buys our products and services?	All companies with employees was the starting point but on examination we found that not all small company owners had enough of a budget to pay for training or wanted the specialist training being offered.
What type of people are they?	Small and medium companies with between ten and 150 employees who want to improve their employees' skill level to increase their efficiency at their jobs or take over from a colleague when the colleague was away from their work. These companies are in the Business to Consumer (B2C) segment.
Who is already selling our products and services to these customers?	There are a number of competitors in the marketplace of various sizes from multinational to individual freelance trainers (who mainly supplied via medium sized training providers).
Are the competitors selling to the micro, small, medium or large companies?	The competitors were mainly focused on the large business sector. We found that there were only a few companies offering specialist training to the small and medium business sector and no-one developing specifically to the micro business.
Is there a sector that is not being serviced?	The small and medium business sector was not clearly catered for and, after some primary research and test trading, we found the micro business sector would or could not afford to pay for training, preferring to learn from online sources.
Should we specialize in a particular market sector?	We decided to focus on the small and medium business market.
Who else is selling into the chosen sector?	We identified a number of trainers who offered the same specialist training. The client sent some of their staff on a number of these training courses to investigate their presentation and content. During breaks they spoke to the other delegates, gathering information on the perceptions of the training.

Question	Answer
What types of companies are buying in that sector?	There was an eclectic mix of sectors with each course they went on. Further examination of the competitors' websites showed that their clients were also from mixed sectors.
Who purchases the most in that sector?	We reviewed the list of companies in the client's own database and the competitor information that had been gathered. The target clients were mainly manufacturers or resellers. We also looked at business organizations and groups such as chambers of commerce and business clubs who had large memberships the same as our target segments. These were also targeted to act as resellers for the client. They provide the delegates and the client provides the training. These organizations were also able to generate income for their organizations whilst the client did not have to advertise and promote the training events.

Table 2

If you have sales information, set up a table or similar analysis to map out which companies or types of customer have purchased from you and what products they favour. Try to identify what industries or segments they have come from and what was the process you went through to sell to them. Some of this may seem obvious to you or you may think you know this already, but it can surprising when you actually look at the figures. In the many years I have been advising businesses I am always astonished at how few analyse their records to find out where most of their sales actually come from or calculate who is the most profitable customer; instead most rely on their 'gut' feeling, believing that they know their business better than anyone.

What products or services?

Bear in mind that the products or services that sell best in the physical world are not necessarily the ones that will sell best online. The same applies to customers and customer behaviour. Those customers who currently represent your most profitable may not necessarily purchase online. For example, a high street specialist food retailer, such as a delicatessen, might sell freshly cut meats or speciality breads on a daily basis to customers who live locally, or call during their lunch break or on their way home from work. This may represent the largest part of the shop's turnover. The online customer profile and purchases, however, might be quite different. They would be likely not to live locally and may purchase items that had a longer shelf life or would travel well, such as pâtés or preserves that were tinned or in jars; perhaps whole cured meats as opposed to sliced. This needs to be taken into account in conjunction with your sales figures and forecasts.

In general, though not a hard and fast rule, there are types of products that sell well online.

- Digital products that by their nature are effectively delivered directly to the customer. These include software, music and, less often, video downloads, as well as information in the form of reports and so on.

- Standard products, by which I mean things that are the same wherever you buy them with little or no variation. These would include books, CDs, DVDs, toys, household appliances such as washing machines and kettles, and electronic items from mobile phones to computers.

- Transactional type products, such as booking for hotels, holidays and travel, tickets for sports, theatre or other events, insurance and financial services.

- Distant products that are not available in the customers' area.

Of course, these are also the most competitive areas for online selling.

If you sell more than one type of product and are targeting more than one distinct type of customer, you might need to consider a multiple website approach. Note that this is not necessarily the solution for everyone; this approach works for some companies, but if used inappropriately it could result in the customer being very confused and work against the business. Some large companies have multiple websites that have developed as a result of organic growth and a departmentalized approach, or reflect how the company is structured internally.

I recently met someone who works for a large multinational where the company is currently maintaining 70+ websites that were set up over a period of probably more than a decade. It must have seemed logical and a good idea each time another website was set up to promote a new product or to provide information to the customers of a specific division. However, they now have the unenviable task of rationalizing and integrating these sites into a structure that targets their customers, rather than is focused on their business.

Not long ago I worked with a company in the reverse position. They are a multi-million turnover company who were trying to market three completely different types of product from one website. From the company's point of view they are related; however, from the customers' point of view they are not. The products are for different markets, with different end users. Sales records showed that virtually no customers bought more than one type of product. Even though the website seemed well optimized for the search engines, they were not succeeding in getting onto the first page of results for any of their products or services.

The site was trying to cover all of the different products in an integrated way and, although they were getting a large number of visitors to the site, the visitors were being confused when they arrived at the site; virtually none was being converted into customers. There was so much information on the different products that it was difficult to glean separate information on any one of them.

To resolve the problem they followed my advice and published three separate websites, each covering one specific business sector. The customers can now find what they are looking for and the three websites have higher results for each target customer type. More website visitors are being converted into customers, and enquiries and orders are up.

What questions do I need to answer?
The questions below are listed for guidance and represent a starting point or reference only:

The Business to Business market (B2B)
- What is the company size?

- What is their approximate turnover?

- How many people do they employ?

- Where are they based?

- Where are their customers (the end users)?

- What do they supply?

- What is the cost of their products?

- How does this cost compare with their competitors?

- Who are their decision makers?

- How old are the decision makers?

- What is their gender?

- What is their corporate mission?

The Business to Consumer market (B2C)

There are far more questions that need answering. The marketplace is much bigger and therefore needs to be broken down into greater detail, narrowing the scope of your advertising and promotion. More questions need to be answered about the target groups to focus on the ideal target customer.

- What is their age group?

- What is their income level?

- What is their disposable income?

- What is their occupation?

- What is their gender?

- Where do they live?

- Do they own their house? What type of house?

- Are they married?

- Do they have children? How many? How old are they?

- What sports do they support?

- What are their hobbies?

- What is their educational level?

Again this is not a definitive list of questions. There are many other questions that can be asked to develop your target customer profile. The more you know, the more accurate the profile is. While there will be some limitations such as time and budget, it is important to collect as much data as possible, ensuring that the data collected is relevant.

What do you SELL – what do customers BUY?

The viewpoints of a business from the inside and outside are often quite different. It can be quite a surprise to compare how the business sees itself in terms of what it sells, what its products are, or what its intentions may be, with how its customers see it or why they buy from it.

Let's look at a town centre coffee shop. (There are many of these, both independent businesses and franchises.) When you go into the coffee shop, your reason for doing so might be obvious: you go in to buy coffee; or tea; perhaps lunch or one of those great toasted sandwiches; maybe just because you need to have a sit down; to meet friends; because they don't mind pushchairs and will heat up your baby's bottle or maybe because you like the atmosphere in there. Hmm . . . so maybe even though it is a coffee shop, it's not just to buy coffee, is it? This kind of knowledge allows the owner of the coffee shop to differentiate from his competitors, it is this insight that has made the coffee shop chains that you see in every town so successful. They know they are not selling coffee, they are selling an experience. By finding out who represents the largest spend and who your most profitable customers are, it is possible to adjust the offering (what the shop offers for sale) to suit.

In 2006 almost 12 per cent of UK adults were members of a sports club, gym or fitness club. When surveyed, people said they joined these organizations for health and fitness purposes, lifestyle choices and social contact. They like to see themselves as the 'kind of person who goes to the gym' or they care about their personal image or are safeguarding their health or just trying to lose weight. Most health clubs sell their membership as an annual contract with a monthly subscription payment – and are very good at doing so. While they are providing gym and sports facilities, largely their sales efforts are targeted directly at selling subscriptions. They have secondary sales of course, often food or sports clothes but mainly they sell subscriptions.

Hotels sell different things to different types of customers. Basically, they sell rooms with beds and bathrooms, food and drink and a place to consume them. The customers, however, perceive this in different ways. Many business travellers who are road-weary will often use the same hotel chain again and again wherever they go because it might not be the best but they know exactly what they are going to get, so they are buying a substitute home, a place that is familiar and they feel secure when away from their real home (hence the success of the chains Travel Inn and Travelodge). Holiday travellers might make choices for completely different reasons: perhaps because it represents very good value for money and they can ill afford to travel anyway but are determined to despite their tight budget. Other holidaymakers might splash out once a year and fulfil their lifestyle desires that they cannot possibly afford every day: 5 stars, room service, spa treatments, the celebrity lifestyle (or so they perceive it).

Think hard about what you are selling. How is it perceived from the point of view of your customers? This can be the key to being customer focused. What are your customers buying and why?

Proctor and Gamble, who make the market-leading Fairy Liquid, have been selling a chemical compound that is used to wash dishes for 45 years. Interesting that much of their advertising imagery is about perfect families, soft-focus lifestyle and, of course, soft hands. Do you remember the song: "Hands that do dishes, can feel soft as your face, with mild green Fairy Liquid"? They don't use the rhyme or song any more, Fairly Liquid isn't always green and comes in lemon, antibacterial, apple blossom, floral breeze and purple herbal and now lime and lemongrass, pink grapefruit and garden mint. Most bizarrely in my kitchen as I am writing this, there is a bottle of Fairy Liquid called 'passion flower storm' (what is that all about?). All of this may be so, but nearly all of the people over about 25 who we surveyed can sing the song!

Industry jargon – what do your customers call your products or services?

When you are in an industry or are close to the business, you are familiar on a day to day basis with all the industry terms and jargon for your services and products. All those acronyms relating to the industry trip off your tongue when you describe the features of your products, stock or services.

What about your customers? Are they knowledgeable of the terminology used in your industry, or do they describe your products and services in a different way? Are they buying the same thing that you think they are? These are important issues to consider.

In a Business to Business market you might be fairly sure that the purchaser will be aware of the terminology that you use. However, be very careful about this. I recently worked for a client on a telecoms company website. I was given a list of terms and key phrases that the client wanted to use. Reading through the list I raised my concerns about some of the items and words proposed. In particular: 'least cost routing', 'VOIP' and 'PBX'.

They had confirmed to me that they were clear on who they were selling to: according to the size or type of business, this might be the business owners or directors, project managers, IT managers, etc. I questioned as to whether these customers would necessarily know these terms. IT specialists within a company may be familiar with them if they had been given the project to improve the telecoms in a company and had researched the telecoms industry, but it was still unlikely that they would be as conversant with these terms as a telecoms specialist. A small amount of research confirmed this was true; we could not assume that they would.

I then asked if they were clear on who were the decision makers for previous sales. The response was that they were mostly company owners, managing directors and finance directors. I also enquired if they had identified their customers' main interest in the services being offered. The response was that they all were interested in cost reduction, a more efficient telephone system and to make the company look bigger by introducing an exchange. We looked at these influencers and reworded the keyword list (more about keywords later) to accommodate the features in a non-jargon way. This has proved to be very successful and they are now enjoying a higher conversion rate of visitors into enquiries.

Pay attention if you are in an industry that is littered with jargon. Maybe you do not think that you use jargon and believe that the terminology that you use every day is obvious. Ask some people outside your industry; ask the types of people you are selling to. To be confident in using the jargon, you need to confirm conclusively – by research – that your industry terms are in everyday use by your customers.

I recently encountered a government website that has a three-letter acronym halfway through the first sentence on the home page. I don't know what this term means and I therefore have no idea what the page is about as the meaning of all the following sentences relies on this understanding, and the page gives no contextual clues. I can also find no explanation of this term in the website. I am sure that this is a term that the most junior of employees in that department is familiar with, but since I represent the group the website is targeted at, clearly not the customers.

In the interests of a random survey I asked everyone who came into my office over the course of a week, including the postman, if they knew what it meant and only one did (and he used to work in the public sector).

Compile a list of terms from your business or industry and go out and ask some people who are not in your industry if they know what they mean. In my industry, SEO means Search Engine Optimization but when we worked on a public sector contract some years ago SEO meant Special Executive Officer. Take care with the assumptions you make, ask your customers. You might be surprised.

Research research research

If you do not identify the target audience for your business's products or services, or understand your customers' needs, you are unlikely to be able (except by accident) to capture their attention when they arrive at your website. By understanding their terms of reference and their language, you will be able to empathize with their ideals and make a connection. Even though this may be in opposition to your current concept of your business, or go against your own values, we have to remember who the website is for: your customers.

5

WHAT ARE YOUR COMPETITORS DOING?

At the end of the Second World War, Japan was desperate to rebuild its economy. The country was determined to build an economy that would be sustainable, provide employment and be the envy of the world. With the help of Western Governments, the Japanese sent their brightest and best students to universities and businesses in Europe and the USA; to learn the methods and secrets of the leading industrial nations of their time. Those students studied hard, learning all they could. On their return to Japan their education was put to good use, introducing the practices, principles and processes they had learned. They realized that things could be improved further by building on their new-found knowledge; by developing their techniques the student became the master. Since the early 1980s it has been Japanese processes and principles that have been the main source of business improvement as British and American manufacturing companies have been trying desperately to catch up.

It could be said that the Japanese won the war by stealth, not force – by learning and understanding how the economies of their former enemies worked, and by improving on them to become world leaders in industry. The sixth century Chinese war strategist Sun

Tzu[1] proposed that you should: "Understand your enemy, find his weaknesses and destroy him where he is weak." I am obviously not advocating that you adopt this literally; but by applying an interpretation of these principles to your business, you can help it on the path to success.

Research

Unless you are the leaders in your market (which is unlikely as if so you would probably not be reading this book), there will always be companies who are bigger or more successful than yours. By studying their actions and activities you can benefit from their knowledge – not necessarily by copying directly, but by observation and the careful selection of what may benefit your specific situation.

As with customer research, we have two paths to sourcing information: primary research and secondary research. It is important at this point to consider if you have time for these activities and whether you can assign this task to one of your colleagues (if you have any) or should consider contracting an agency or third party provider.

Direct or indirect

Competitors come in two types: direct and indirect. The direct competitors are easier to identify; they are the ones who *sell exactly the same* as you do, and to the *same customers*.

Indirect competitors can be a little more difficult to pinpoint and might involve some creative thinking. Indirect competitors are competing for *the same spend* as you from the same customer profiles but do not necessarily provide exactly the same products or services.

To understand this better, if you sell crisps and potato-based

---

1. If you are interested in Chinese War strategies you can find information and links related to Sun Tzu at: http://en.wikipedia.org/wiki/Sun_Tzu.

snacks, then another company that sells crisps is your direct competitor. A company that sells nuts, or snack bars, or chocolate is also your competitor but indirectly; it does not sell exactly the same thing as you, but competes for the same customer spend. In the newsagents, corner shop or supermarket, the goods are often displayed side-by-side and compete for the attention of the customer, and consequently for the money in their purse or pocket.

Take transport as an example. To reach your destination you might drive, take a train or fly. Each of these industries has direct competitors within them but indirectly they all compete for the travelling public's spend.

Which airline do you fly with? Which car do you purchase or lease, and from which company? If hired, which car hire company do you use? A car hire company should be interested in what other car hire companies are up to – are they cutting their prices, offering incentives or just being better at what they do? But such a company also needs to be aware of improved public transport links or a change in the cost of owning a car.

This applies clearly in the tourism industry where there is a vast array of indirectly competing activities available to the tourist from museums to theme parks. All of those tourism businesses are chasing the same tourist spend whether it is the Pound, Euro or Dollar.

Whatever industry you are in and whoever you are targeting, it is likely that you will have both direct and indirect competitors. As they are after the same money, it pays for you to make investigations into their activities as far as is possible and be informed of what is going on.

Researching offline

Newspapers, journals, trade shows and business organizations such as the Chamber of Commerce[2] can provide access to a vast

---

2. www.chamberonline.co.uk

array of information on your competitors. However, it can be a daunting task to try to assimilate such a plethora of information. You have to be selective; keep files on each of the competitor organizations thus building a picture of their activities. Competitors' promotional brochures and documents, their press releases and the commentary from industry journalists will contribute to the collection. For those whom you identify to be your primary competition, it may be worth accessing information from Companies House[3] to gain insights on their finances.

Researching online
The online environment opens up a whole new world of access to information. It can take just a few moments of looking at your competitor's website to find information on the company, how well they are promoting themselves online, and what and where they are targeting their efforts. It is also possible (although not always easy) to identify their target customers by interpreting their use of terminology and key phrases. There are websites online that offer information services on companies; these include Dun and Bradstreet[4], who monitor the financial status of companies, to credit reference agencies that monitor the creditworthiness of companies and individuals in the UK.

Online services such as Meltwater News[5] track business names online and in magazines, journals and newspapers. If you want to track the promotional and press releases of a competitor company, you can subscribe to their services. Alternative, less expensive options are available, such as the service provided by Google. While Google Alerts is a free service, it is obviously restricted to the internet.

---

3. www.companies-house.gov.uk
4. www.dnb.com
5. www.meltwaternews.com

The competitor's website

Studying a competitor's website is easy and provides an important source of information. Remember that you should do so with an open mind. Depending on your approach or experience, it is tempting either to take an automatically critical approach; or to think that since they are doing more business than you, their website must be an exemplar of good practice. Of course, none of this is necessarily true and all the information you gather must be assessed in context and with a measure of caution. It can take years of study and experience to be able to observe and interpret effectively the information available online in order to get a clear view of the good and bad points of a website.

Searching on key phrases

Use the keywords and phrases that you define for your products and services (more on this in Chapter 6, Selecting Keywords to Target Your Customers) to conduct searches in Google. Check out the first page or two of results. This is both an efficient way of finding out who your online competitors are, and of investigating their activities. Their positioning (in the results list) and their website can tell you a lot.

Questions to ask yourself as you look at their website might include:

- Are they direct or indirect competitors?

- What products are they promoting?

- Do they appear to be targeting the same market sector as you?

- What is the language of the website – is it targeted at the professional or end user? (More on this in Chapter 12, The Language of the Customer.)

- Where are they based – is it local to your business? What is their geographical scope, does this overlap with your business's scope?

- What information do they display about themselves?

- Are there prices or price indicators on the site?

- Are they focused on themselves or on their customers – do they show their mission statements or include pictures of their main staff?

- Is the website up to date or clearly maintained regularly – if there is a news page with news items on it, are these current?

- Do they have a list of customers? (Could these be yours?)

- What is your first impression of their website, is it easy to use? (Try not to be too opinionated about this.)

Source code

We will look into more detail on the source code of a website in Chapter 7, Now You Have Your Keywords, Where do They Go?, but at this stage, it is worth looking at your competitors' source code to see if they have made any effort to optimize their website.

Gaining access to the source code is usually quite a simple process although it does vary according to the type of browser you are using. If you are using Internet Explorer (the most common browser) 'right-click' (the mouse) on the screen of the competitor's website and look for the menu choice 'View Source'. This will open a new window – usually Notepad – containing the source code for the website. See Fig. 8.

Don't be alarmed about all the code and gobbledegook that you see and the fact that it is unlikely that you will know what it all means; it is quite possible that neither did the person who built this website. It is more than likely that he used some software that created a lot of this code automatically.

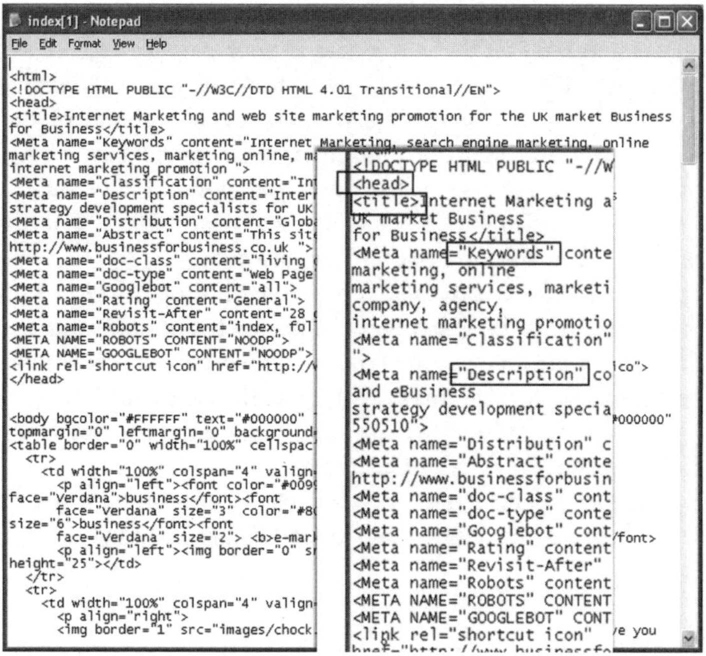

Fig. 8 A web page's source code.

We are interested in the section, usually at the top, known as the 'head code' and which can be found between the entries <head> and </head>. These represent the start and finish points of this section. The head code consists of a variety of instructions, including information that the browser uses to display the website and what the search engines use to record information. Here you will find the title of the web page, the description that is displayed in the search engine results and sometimes a list of keywords.

The first check is to look at the source code of the home page: have they completed a title, description and keyword list? If not, then it is an initial indication of lack of optimization. Now check the title, description and keyword list for the other pages in the site. If they are there, is the information the same as on the home page or is it different?

If the information is the same for each page, we can make an assumption that the whole site is poorly optimized. To be effective, each page should have its own title, description and set of keywords and phrases relevant to the content of the page. If the information is missing or is the same on each page of the site, we can assume the site is not optimized and the site owner is not taking full advantage of the opportunities that the internet offers for promotion of the business.

The next check is to look at the keywords, or description if there are any. If there are, you can keep a list of these and use them as an indicator to the type of keywords that you should be thinking of when you start to compile your own keyword list. (This is dealt with in the next chapter, Selecting Keywords to Target your Customers.)

On that subject, it may be worth checking your own site to see if the title, description and keywords are included.

Secrets in the search engines
On receiving an email from a potential supplier I was curious to find out more about him before I considered his business. Even though he had not included contact details (only his name and a reply email address), I was able to find out a great deal about him.

A search in Google produced a considerable amount of information including personal data on the individual – far too much for his comfort. Within a few minutes of receiving his promotional newsletter I had phoned the sender to warn him of his online situation; I was concerned that this information could be used to steal his identity. From a single search I was able to give him his date of birth, home address details, political allegiance and membership number and renewal date for a private sports club he belonged to.

It might have been possible (if I had persisted with further research) to do a credit check on this person and potentially identify his bank details. As we use the internet, joining various organizations, registering and subscribing to websites and social networks, we leave a trail of personal information online. Much of this is historically in the public domain and, unless this is secured, the search engines are able to interrogate and pick it up, providing it as results for searches.

One of the factors that increases your 'findability' on the internet is any degree of individuality. You might think therefore that, if your name is John Smith or some other name that is in common use, there is little likelihood of anyone pinpointing you as an individual amongst all the other John Smiths.

However, consider your email address john.smith@ awebsiteaddress.co.uk. By definition, your email address is unique; and can be identified as such wherever you have posted it. Search Engines are constantly cataloguing information and storing it, ready for retrieval by a searcher. The same applies to any information on your business and, of course, that of your competitors.

Whatever information you have posted (whether deliberately or unknowingly) or whatever someone else has posted about you, if those websites have open access or are unsecured, then a search for that information can potentially be found quite easily.

What competitors wouldn't want you to know
The internet offers a whole new world of opportunity for complaint. There are countless forum boards dedicated to poor service that have been built by disgruntled customers. With a little basic knowledge or access to software tools, one can easily be set up to condemn the company that gave them a poor service.

A few examples of these types of site are:

- http://www.ripoffreport.com/   a website for people to post bad experiences with companies.

- http://walmartwatch.com   a specific campaign to show the bad effects of the supermarket on small towns in America.

- http://www.reviewdo.co.uk   a site set up for people to review companies they have done business with. This has positive as well as negative results but it seems most of the reviews are negative.

- A simple search on the words, "Don't use this company" (including the quotation marks to search on that complete phrase) can often reveal more than a few examples of the damage that this type of website review can do to a business.

Try searching on a company name (in inverted commas) followed by the phrase "confidential information" or others from the list below. For example: "ABC enterprises" confidential information.

- Confidential information

- Intelligence report

- Legal case

- Court case

- Disgruntled customers

- Unhappy customers

- Customer complaints

- Don't shop at "Competitor's name"

- Customer's revenge

This can reveal (among other things) if your competitors have been involved in a legal case. If they have ever been prosecuted for health and safety or other issues, as court and legal cases are in the public domain this information will surface in a search. I recently found out quite accidentally that a company I was looking for (and have made a variety of purchases from in the past), has been the subject of a number of prosecutions for breaches of health and safety regulations. I was only looking for their phone number and hours of business. Have they ever upset one of their customers over poor service?

Of course, not all searches will bring results. Of course, you need to treat this information with some caution, unless you can be sure of the source (such as a government site). Remember that for any business, in any type of industry, there are likely to be some people who are not happy with the service they have received and decide to get their own back!

A man who was unhappy with a charge on his phone bill and the lack of service or response he received from his telecoms supplier recently (at the time of writing) posted a video of himself talking about the complaint on YouTube. Now he is entitled to make a complaint, and there is nothing stopping him from posting information on YouTube that is true, but even though he has now apparently received an apology and a refund, it is likely that the video is still on YouTube and may stay there for a long time. Add to this the PR he had on the TV news and magazine programmes. As an overall effect this can represent a lot of damage to a business, particularly if it was a small one.

Pause for thought

Hang on a minute. If you are searching for this information on your competitors, then don't you think it is worth looking up your own name and your company online? There may be a few surprises in the results, so what can you do about it? You may need to formulate a plan of action:

• Personal information posted on networking or social web sites in your profile page can be removed by rewriting your profile.

- Public domain information from legal issues cannot be removed but there are ways of putting these out of the usual range of vision. Research has shown that most people do not look beyond page 3 of results (the first 30 results) so if you can move the information further down then it is less likely to be noticed.

- The publication of articles online and posting on other websites like forum boards and directories will eventually push the unwanted websites lower in the search results.

- The same process can be used to move references to forum boards and websites set up by unhappy customers who wish to discredit your business.

- If you find websites that have defamatory or libellous information relative to your business (and you can prove this), you can contact the search engine in writing and ask for those sites or references to be removed from their listing. You can also approach the hosting company to take the site down.

Differentiate or die

The commercial world is so competitive that in order to succeed and be effective you have to ensure that your business is differentiated from your competitors. This is now accepted as a key success factor for business of any size.

Much is talked about 'unique selling points' or 'propositions' (USPs). I would question how many businesses actually have something that is unique. I would say that there are probably very few; and by definition would include those that are successfully marketing patented products. Even these are temporary (lasting the life of the patent which in the UK is 20 years) or the period of time taken for someone to come up with a better solution or option (which is usually less).

'Emotional selling points' (ESPs) and more recently 'social selling points' (SSPs) have both been topical subjects. These may now be more relevant to the business of today, particularly one that proposes to trade online.

An emotional selling point is something that involves or invokes emotional or irrational purchasing decisions, rather than considered logical actions. This may sound rather rash, but it has been found (by extensive research) that many types of goods are effectively marketed in this way. Have you ever stood in a shop or looked at a catalogue and thought, "I must have that new mobile phone/shoes/product-I-don't-really-need/or whatever"? If so, you are not alone.

For example, it seems that only a few years ago, if someone was purchasing a new kettle (as kettles were relatively expensive and would be expected to last decades) he would go about the purchase carefully, considering if it had an appropriate capacity or was well made and so on. Nowadays, it is more likely that someone will be browsing in an electrical superstore and say, "Wow! Just look at that fabulous blue/silver/bullet-shaped/sexy kettle, it would be great in our new kitchen, let's have it now!" And he'd buy it with no further thought.

The increase in supply of consumer goods has a lot to do with this, as well as our higher disposable income and reduction in the relative cost of such goods. Other obvious examples of the use of ESPs include: charities that show pictures of sick or stricken animals and children on TV; or anything that 'tugs at the heart strings'; items that persuade parents through guilt or desire to provide the best possible for their offspring also use this type of leverage.

Social selling points are a more recent phenomenon and have become very common in the last year or so. They rely on the buyers' social or moral conscience and their use is clearly increasing. Wherever you see references to: 'carbon neutral', 'reducing your carbon footprint', 'global warming', 'fairtrade' and so on, where products and services have associated themselves with being 'kind to the planet', 'green' or similar, then a social selling point is being applied.

Finding out information on your competitors will enable you to identify many different aspects of their business activities. From their public profile you can make judgements to identify their customers, their market places and their marketing activities. Why would you want this information? What could you possibly gain from knowing what your competitors are doing to raise their market position or increase their sales?

Understanding the weaknesses of your competitors can give you opportunities to be better than them. How you deal with this information is up to you. One approach is to develop a strategy that enables your business to find the market that gives you customers and avoids a head to head competition for the sale. As a business you can decide to develop in an area that the competitor has missed, or gain benefit by observing mistakes that a competitor has made and learning from them.

Whatever action you decide to take, I always say that you do not have to destroy a competitor's business to build yours. Bear this in mind as you take action on the information you gather.

6

SELECTING KEYWORDS TO TARGET YOUR CUSTOMERS

The old adage about looking for a needle in a haystack takes on a completely new scale when it comes to the internet. It is considered difficult if not impossible to find the proverbial needle, as the haystack is too large or complex to do so. But how about looking for a reference or subject, based on a word or phrase search, in a place where it is estimated that there are more than 100 trillion words.[1]

I often ask people attending my seminars what it is that they find the most frustrating when searching the internet for information. The most common response is their inability to find the information, product or service that they are looking for.

So whose fault is this? Is it the users for not typing the correct search term – are they using an appropriate keyword or phrase to find the information or product? Or does the problem lie with the website (and therefore the owners, managers and developers who are responsible for the

---

1. There is no definitive record of this and as it changes every second there is unlikely to be. This estimate was made at the Google developer day at the San Jose Convention Center. Peter Norvig, the Director of Research at Google, made an educated guess that the internet is a repository for more than 100 trillion words, as reported by Dean Takahashi on the 'Tech Talk blog' on 31/05/2007. As Peter Norvig is an American, a trillion is a 1 followed by 12 zeros, or 100,000,000,000.

website's setup and maintenance) for not containing the terms that people are looking for?

Or is it (more likely) a combination of both? If the websites are not optimized for the search engines, then the search engines will not be able to list them effectively. Worse, if a website is not optimized for the customers (what they are looking for; what things are called in the customers' language, and therefore what kind of terms they are likely to search on), then they will also not be listed in the search engine results.

And therein lies the rub.

In many cases, this results from the state of the web design industry, and that of website optimization, being so poor. Businesses are losing out on millions of potential customers; those who may be seeking to purchase from their websites or use their websites' services, but simply cannot find them and so give up or go elsewhere.

Interestingly, those conducting the searches – the users or customers – invariably blame themselves for their lack of skill, knowledge or experience in using the internet.

As a website owner you can gain advantage or even beat your competitors with this knowledge. By focusing on optimizing your website for the keywords that the customers are using, you can achieve higher search engine listings for those search terms. In Chapter 5, we looked at the websites of our competitors. We could see from them what our competitors are doing – hoping to get or achieving high listings. We can apply this research to help get ahead of the competition and optimize our site, hopefully beating them to the top of the search results page and the customer.

Of course, there is a lot more to getting sales online than optimizing your website so that it appears in search engine listings for the things your potential customer is looking for. But it is one of the essential factors to online success; if no-one can find your website, no-one can buy from you.

The secret behind a successful website – in terms of search engine promotion – is the use of the right keywords and phrases. These are used to get your business website in front of the customers when they are looking for your products and services. The keywords you choose to target are paramount to its success.

It is important to understand at this point that you cannot rely on your potential customers to speak the same language as you. The time spent researching the customer profile and the language of the customer pays off when it comes to predicting what keywords to use. This is also discussed in Chapter 12, The Language of the Customer.

If you have identified multiple customer profiles and have, or are, setting the website up to accommodate this, then you need to note that the broader and less specific the terminology, the more difficult it is to get into the top ten as there is more competition for those terms. For example: if you are targeting customers who search on the term 'plumber' it is much harder to get in the top ten for this term than if you are targeting customers who are searching on the term 'plumbing installation services London'. At the time of writing, a UK search on 'plumber' produces 1,780,000 results; a similar search on the term 'plumbing installation services' produces only 455. Simple logic prevails here. If you aim and manage to be in the top 20 per cent relative to your competitors in the first example, then you are going to appear somewhere in the first 35,000 pages of results. Not particularly effective. In the second example, you are in the first 90 listings. Not necessarily on page one, but still findable. Add a town or city to this 'plumbing installation services London' then there are just nine results. You will definitely be on page one.

If you have multiple customer profiles or offer products or services that target completely different types of customer, then it is worth considering the development of more than one website. This can then be optimized for the different customer profiles that you have identified in your research. Each site would include a focused set of key phrases which can be targeted at one of the customer profiles, enhancing your opportunities to reach all parts of your market. This can also apply if your customers are split between consumers and businesses: consider having a site specifically for consumers and a second website for the trade. In the past, cost would have prohibited this strategy, but the price of website development is reducing as the industry becomes more competitive, so this is becoming a viable option.

Entry points

A shop in the high street will probably have only one entrance – the front door. A larger store may have two or three entrances. A website, however, has multiple entrances or entry points. In fact (unless your site is set up specifically in such a way as not to allow the search engines to list anything but the home page – which would be unusual) your website has potentially as many entry points as it has pages, like a building having an external door into every single room.

Research shows that over 60 per cent of entries into a website from a search engine results page are directly to pages other than the home page. This kind of deep-linking, as it is called, is a good thing as it directs users straight to the page holding the information they are looking for.

If visitors get straight to the page with the information, product or service they need, it saves them time, it keeps them happy and they will be more inclined to purchase with you, whatever your offering may be. Conversely, they get very irritated if they follow a search engine results link for something specific to a website only to find that they have landed on the home page and then have to search or browse through the site to find the item or information they are looking for.

In order to link to the correct page, it is crucial that you do not just optimize the home page of your website, but deal with every single page that you would wish a search engine to list, with each page having its own title, description and keyword information.

Your home page is the most important, of course, and if you are limited to one website that targets more than one type of customer (e.g. domestic and trade buyers), or if you sell more than one type of product or service, then the home page optimization has to accommodate all of them. It is worth considering the fact that if you try to make anything serve two purposes – a chair that is also a step-stool; a table that is also a storage chest – you will have to accept compromise. The chair may not be so elegant or comfortable; you might have to remove any items that are on that table in order to access the storage. It is the same with a website. If you are targeting two types of customers with one website, you will never be able to target them as well as if you were targeting them separately.

Keywords and phrases

Fig. 9 The 'title bar' (coloured bar at the top of the screen) with 'title'.

Keywords and phrases are going to be implemented in a variety of places. The initial concern is in the meta names (a section of the HTML that is not seen by the user), specifically in the 'title', 'description' and 'keyword' tags. The 'title' is the text that is seen in the 'title bar' (the coloured bar at the top of the screen – see Fig. 9), and is also the first line of information in the search engine listings followed by the description (see Fig. 10).

Keywords are also used in other situations as well as throughout the content of the site. Don't worry too much about the detail of this as it will be discussed further in the next chapter.

Before any optimization can be carried out, we need to be

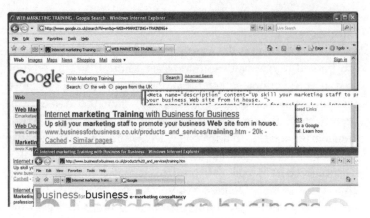

Fig. 10 The 'title' appearing as first line of information in the search engine listings.

clear on whom we are optimizing for – who is the customer that we are targeting?

In this example, we will initially look at the business or professional buyer. In this case, our worked example is targeting the professional photographer. This customer is effectively a B2B buyer and is more likely to have industry knowledge, understand technical terms and to be more specific, quoting the product codes instead of, or as well as, the brand names (which would be more likely from the consumer). This example could easily be adapted to meet the needs of the amateur photographer – the B2C buyer.

Our scenario: A professional photographer has been browsing photographic magazines and has seen the latest model of a digital camera featured. He already uses equipment by this manufacturer and is keen to have the latest version and the added bonus of better functionality and higher resolution.

Our objective: establish a set of keywords that will effect-ively target this customer. Prioritize which are to be used on the home page. (The others will be used on more specific product pages.)

Our task is to develop a list of keywords that coincides with the keywords or phrases that this type of customer would be likely to use. (When you are carrying out this exercise on your own business, the research and customer profiling discussed in Chapter 4, Who is the Website for Anyway?, will provide guidance. Chapter 12, The Language of the Customer, will also contribute some insights.)

We surveyed numerous photographers, from photo-journalists to fine-art photographers, professionals of many years experience to students, to see what they would be most likely to type into a search engine. The most common response was manufacturer's name followed by product code (which they would have obtained from the article or advert in our scenario), alternatively, brand name followed by the term 'professional digital camera'. This will guide us in creating a list of keywords and phrases.

In addition, we need to identify the top selling brands in the market; in this scenario they are well established. For the purposes of this example, we are using Olympus, Canon, Fuji, Sony and Nikon. (This example obviously assumes that we sell all these brands.)

We also need to be aware of what our competitors are doing, as discussed in Chapter 5, What are Your Competitors Doing? The last thing is to be aware of current activities, including any advertising campaigns that any of the manu-facturers are engaged in, also any current PR that might be happening such as items being featured on TV shows or similar.

So the first activity is to list the keywords. Once you have a first draft, it will need to be reviewed, and there are tools online that can help with this. These tools are mainly to help you assess your potential keyword choices, to see if they are often requested by users searching (potential customers), or to see how many results are returned in a Google search. This shows the number of pages that are including the term; in other words, if they are popular with other websites (potential competitors).

Table 3 gives a sample of the information for search requests and search results. It has been sorted into search request (users' search) order.

It is interesting to discover that 290 people searched on 'discount digital cameras' (item 5 in the list) more than twice the number that searched on 'cheap digital cameras' (131 in item 10).

In addition to the obvious brand names, it can be difficult to think up all combinations of key phrases. While the tools available on the internet are mainly to help you assess your potential keyword choices, as above, some of them also suggest alternatives that can help with your choices.

To access online keyword tools and services
Firstly, if you haven't done it already sign up for an account with Google[2]. This will not cost anything and they provide a number of functions and tools to help you improve your website. They are easy to set up; simply follow the online instructions. The ones that you will probably find useful include:

• Put your information on Google.

• Enhance your website.

• Increase your productivity.

When you have an account, register for the AdWords program. This is on the same page and called, 'Advertise on Google with AdWords'. This is free of charge to set up and carries no obligations. You will only be charged once the program is activated. The reason for using this service, even if you do not intend to activate the adwords, is that the service provides a tool to find out how many times someone requested

---

2. Go to www.google.co.uk/services/ to find these.

Keyword	Search request (users in the previous 30 days)	Google search (number of results returned)
digital cameras	2584	109,000,000
canon cameras	710	8,010,000
canon digital cameras	398	44,100,000
olympus cameras	359	3,930,000
discount digital cameras	290	12,700,000
fuji digital cameras	281	2,030,000
digital cameras ratings	236	32,500,000
compare digital cameras	230	47,000,000
best digital cameras	212	95,900,000
cheap digital cameras	131	23,000,000
camera lenses	119	5,150,000
digital slr cameras	115	5,090,000
digital camera lenses	36	11,600,000
nikon digital slr cameras	33	3,470,000
canon powershot digital cameras	28	3,420,000
sony digital video cameras	23	54,600,000
nikon slr cameras	16	3,770,000
nikon d50 digital cameras for sale	13	292,000
cheap sony digital cameras	10	68,800,000
digital cameras canon	9	49,400,000
discounted fuji digital cameras	8	1,400,000
lens for nikon digital slr cameras	8	1,960,000
sony digital slr cameras for sale	8	1,510,000
reviews of nikon digital cameras	5	6,420,000
sony digital cameras cheap	5	67,300,000
sony digital cameras lowest prices	5	16,300,000
compare sony digital cameras	4	53,700,000
discount nikon digital cameras	4	12,600,000

Table 3

a search on a given key phrase in the previous month. By searching through this database on proposed keywords and phrases, you will be able to find out the number of times they have been requested. This will give you an idea of the number of people searching on that phrase and therefore the number of potential visitors.

The other data required is the number of results that each search engine returns for your key phrase. The simplest test you can carry out is to go to the search engine page (such as Google), type the search term in the search box and see how many results there are. This immediately indicates how many incidences of a keyword or phrase are currently listed. This, in turn, shows how popular that keyword or phrase is with other websites; in other words, the level of competition for that term. Remember to check the results for the UK only (unless you are targeting a wider geographical scope).

Carry out these checks for each and every keyword, phrase or search term you select for your pages. Use the results to make a qualified judgement on each. The more requested a keyword is, the more likely you are to get visitors as there are more people looking for it. However, the more popular a keyword is with other websites, the harder it will be to get high up in the listings for that keyword, particularly if you are in a very competitive market – like selling digital cameras. Table 3 provides some guidance on the type of information you might record to help you choose.

Not all of the keywords and phrases in Table 3 would be used in the index or home page of the site. There are simply too many, but certainly all of the general ones would be used. The more specific or detailed words and phrases would be used throughout the site on the various pages containing the specific cameras and equipment. Approximately twenty to twenty five words and/or phrases should be drawn from this list (I never said it was going to be easy!). Arrange these in order by relevance of the keywords you predict are the most likely to be searched on, with the most important first.

These will be placed in the title, description, and so on as mentioned earlier and will be covered in detail in the next chapter.

Other factors to consider

It is worth remembering that the number of times a given keyword or phrase is requested could change due to seasonal variations. The most obvious of these is in retail businesses where there is a great increase in demand running up to Christmas. Holiday bookings increase in January and, either as a school holiday approaches, or if we have a rainy summer (which is every year of course). Consultancy and other business services experience a dip in December and August, as these are generally holiday months in business, and an increase in September which is still for many the time to set out on something new, traditionally following the academic year. In addition, look out for news or events hitting the headlines or items featured on news or magazine programmes which can also create an increased interest from searchers. If you are in the position to have direct control over your website and can change the keywords whenever you wish, you can take advantage of the free publicity generated by these occasions.

If your business is related to the local tourist and leisure industry, find out well in advance what events are taking place in your area and use key phrases relating to these activities in plenty of time. Each year there are thousands of local and national events taking place across the country and many businesses fail to take advantage of these. With more people now independently arranging tickets, travel and accommodation, as well as planning itineraries online, even though your business is local, the internet gives you the opportunity for a national or even global reach for the same investment.

Spelling and typos

Spelling mistakes are something that is often overlooked. Within the content of the site we might preach about how important it is to check for spelling and typo errors. (I recently saw a glaring one on a website that was advertising a website copywriting service; I won't be using that company.) However, in the case of keywords, the approach is slightly different. Even though Google kindly offers a 'did you mean this...?' when it doesn't recognize a search term, there are still many people who will miss it. There are so many words and phrases that are habitually spelt incorrectly, together with such a generally poor standard of spelling, supplemented by the hurry most people are in when they are online, it's a wonder that anything ever gets found. Pre-empt this by anticipating spelling mistakes and including them in your keywords if it is an important search phrase.

'Stop' words

It is worth pointing out at this stage that search engines often ignore some words; in particular, those little words that are essential in written English such as 'and' and 'for'. You can see evidence of this on the results page. For example, a search on the key phrase

'professional camera equipment for professional photographers'
results in something like
Results 1 to 10 of 240,000 for
'professional camera equipment professional photographers'

Note the 'for' has been ignored. This is called a 'stop' word. Other common stop words include most prepositions or 'joining' words: and, if, but, the, a, of, to, about, etc. These do change from time to time. The word 'business' used to be a stop word, but was not at the time of writing (but might well be by the time you read this). These words are ignored –

stopped – because if they are included then, due to the way that search logic operates, the number of search results would be too large. It would be reasonable to assume that virtually every single web page on the internet contains the word 'the' or the word 'and'. So if you were to make a search on the key phrase 'The Pig and Whistle' or 'The Coach and Horses' (because you were looking for the phone number of a pub where you wanted to book a table for lunch), then if the words 'the' and 'and' were not ignored, every single web page containing the words 'and' or 'the' would be included in the results. Billions of them!

If your title or description contains one of these words, consider changing it to avoid a waste of characters (as you are limited in characters – more in the next chapter). Of course, this is not always possible and a compromise may be necessary. It makes sense to leave out these words in places where it is only the search engine that is going to see it. However, where sentences are going to be read by the user, they have to make sense. This means that the title and the description fields, which are seen on the search engine results page, need to make sense. We have a situation of compromise here with no clear way of defining exactly what to do. The rule of thumb is: do not use them in the keywords fields, keep stop words to a minimum, only use them to ensure that a sentence makes sense, and consider rearranging sentences or rewording descriptions if you are using stop words a lot.

This brings an added point to this discussion. If the search engines are ignoring these stop words, then if you are choosing a new name for a business, brand or product range, you might consider whether to avoid using those words in the name or certainly where they are an integral part of the name.

Terms and words to avoid

Over the years I have looked at thousands of websites both for research purposes and on behalf of clients. Even though this is relatively well known information in the industry, we still regularly see websites that either have no keywords at all, or ones with titles that contain words such as home page, contact us and services, often the same as the pages' headings. Each of these words or phrases, whilst being descriptive of the content of the page, is so general that they are of no use. How many people will enter the words 'home page', 'contact us' and 'services' into search engines? Virtually no-one does this, so don't use them. Even if someone were to use one of these terms, have a look below at the number of search results. It would be impossible to get to the top of the list.

Google searches at the time of writing:

Search term	UK results	Global results	Comments
Home page	261,000,000	3,590,000,000	Over three billion!
Contact us	320,000,000	3,150,000,000	Over three billion!
Services	202,000,000	1,520,000,000	What services?

Accents and other oddities
A few years ago I needed to find a hotel in a specific area to attend an event. I was attending at quite late notice and so had left it rather late to find somewhere to stay. Eventually on a hotel booking website I came across a country house hotel that was not too far from the event and was available. As always, I looked it up in a variety of places to find information (how to get there, user reviews and so on). Strangely it was nowhere to be found. When I returned to the hotel booking website and followed their link, I found that the problem was with the hotel's own website and their choice of keywords.

It all stemmed from the fact that the name of the hotel has

an accent (on the é). While it is possible to get an accent by using a special character, this is nowhere to be found on the keyboard. The majority of people do not know how to get the character, wouldn't bother when using the internet or in my case, I simply hadn't noticed it when scanning a large amount of dense text on the hotel booking websites.

The title of every page contained the correct name of the hotel, including the accented character. Now a search engine would not be able to see – as a person would – the obvious similarity between an 'e' and 'é'. As far as a computer is concerned it is as different a character as an 'e' and an 'f'. So when a search was conducted without the accented character, the hotel was simply missing from the listings.

When I eventually stayed there, it certainly lived up to the reviews (that I had such difficulty finding). We had a fantastic stay, the food and service was immaculate. I spoke to the owners and suggested that they made some changes to their website. Even though it involved a lot of small but significant changes to their website, it would give them a better chance of being found and greater opportunity for direct bookings (thus saving the commission the hotel booking sites charge for their services). This has now been done and they enjoy the top position for their site.

So, when it comes to choosing your keywords, a lot of the work you have done previously becomes crucial; in particular, an insight into how your customers think and what your competitors are doing.

7

NOW YOU HAVE YOUR KEYWORDS, WHERE DO THEY GO?

Making a cake is a relatively easy task, provided you know how to do it. My mother used to produce a cake for dessert or teatime in between putting the meat in the oven and peeling the vegetables for lunch with no apparent stress. Of course this is like everything else – easy when you know how. She always said that it was not just about what went into the cake, but how you put it together. The butter and sugar had to be beaten together first, the eggs added a little at a time, and the flour sifted over the top and folded in gently. This resulted in a perfect cake every time.

Even though I didn't cook very often, I thought it would be fun to make a cake for her birthday while she was out shopping. I found the recipe and put all the ingredients in a bowl, whisked them up and in the oven they went. Twenty minutes later I had a cake, but nothing like my mother's cake. It was not light and fluffy, it had a strange texture and it only seemed to be half the size of the one she produced. Some of it had stuck to the tin, and I couldn't understand what had gone wrong. I checked the list of ingredients, they were the same as she used; but I had ignored the method. I had not taken the trouble to add the ingredients in the right order. I'd rushed the process and not adhered to the rules. Therefore, the outcome was not as good as it could have been. That said, my mother did appreciate my efforts and ate some cake, but then I was only thirteen at the time.

There are two parts to every recipe: the ingredients list and the method. The previous chapter enabled the ingredients – the keywords and phrases – to be identified and assembled. This chapter deals with the method: what to do with them, where they go and in what order.

It is not possible to deal with keywords and where they go without dipping a toe into the world of the programmer and consequently we will be encountering some technical terms and jargon. You may find it a benefit to have access to the internet so that you can reference some of the content in this chapter with real world examples as you read.

The selection of keywords is only half of the optimization process. In the last chapter we looked at selecting the search terms based on the profile of the customer followed by the analysis of those selected key phrases. Now we look at where these selected keywords are placed in the elements of the page.

Elements for keyword placement

- The website address or URL.

- The page title (that appears in the title bar of the web browser).

- The description (in the meta names used by the search engines to display in the results page).

- The first heading (in the text content of the page).

- The first sentence (in the text content of the page).

- The content of the first paragraph (in the text content of the page).

- The alt text (that is relative to every image).

- The path in the web address of specific pages (e.g. www.bbc.co.uk/food/recipes).

In order for the search engines to provide the best possible results in response to searches, they have developed defensive strategies. These work to prevent some of the practices that webmasters or SEO specialists have used, that try to get their websites to the top of the results for terms that do not relate to the subject that their website covers.

One of these techniques was repeating keywords or phrases many times; this practice is now checked for by Google robots and not treated favourably. So don't try this in your website.

Table 4 shows the current safe limit on the number of characters and keyword repeats you can use in each of the elements in order to ensure that you avoid any penalties.

Using more repeats than the numbers given here may well result in higher or quicker listings in the short term. However, they can also result in being penalized by the search engines or even banned and removed from the listings in the medium to long term.

Short-term gain, long-term pain. Don't be tempted.

Another general point to make is that in any sentence (used in the page title and description as well as the text content in the site) the relevant keyword or phrase should be placed as near to the beginning of the sentence as possible (while still ensuring that the sentence makes sense).

This applies to the search engine results or the rating that search engines give the site (which ultimately determine its positioning in the results). It is also relevant to the way that people use the web when searching for information. Eye-tracking research shows that instead of reading every word as we might expect, most internet users quickly scan the first part of the first line of each paragraph before deciding whether to move on or stop and give more attention to a specific item on

Element	Number of characters	Number of keywords
The website address	N/A	N/A
The title	65	2–3
The description	150	2–3
The first heading	Unlimited but it has to make sense	0
The first sentence	Unlimited but it has to make sense	2
The content of the first paragraph	Unlimited but it has to make sense	3
The alt text	50	2
The path in the web address of specific pages	N/A	N/A

Table 4

the page. Positioning the keywords near the beginning of the sentence and paragraph means that users are more likely to spot them.

For example on a recipe website, instead of writing, "This website contains lots of delicious cake recipes", which has the key phrase 'cake recipes' at the end and uses 45 characters, it is better to restructure the sentence to read, "Cake recipes, delicious and easy to bake." This has only 34 characters, the key phrase now represents the first words in the sentence and we have also managed to get the keywords/phrase 'easy to bake' in as well.

Priority

The search engines prioritize in order of importance:

- The website address or URL.

- The head code HTML and meta names including:

    ○ The page title.

    ○ The description.

    ○ The keywords.

    ○ Plus others detailed below.

- The first heading.

- The first sentence of the first paragraph.

- The alt text.

We are going to deal with each of these elements in turn in order of priority to ensure that the most important is dealt with first.

Website address

It enhances the rating of your business website if the main key phrase is in the website address (URL).

For example, www.professionalcameras.co.uk or www. professionalcameraequipment.co.uk are strong website addresses from a search engine perspective if you wish to benefit from searches on the key phrases 'professional cameras' or 'professional camera equipment'. These have been identified as key phrases and search terms used by professional photographers. A commonly seen choice for URL is the company name, e.g. www.mikesphotography. co.uk. By using the company name, the only key term that will benefit the site is the word photography (which also encompasses the word photograph). Still a strong keyword, but one which is so competitive with 232 million results on a Google search (at the time of writing) that it would be virtually impossible to achieve page one results.

The choice of website address can present some issues if not thought through properly. This is evident in a number of examples which have appeared on the internet:

- Even the Government got it wrong with a recent anti-child-abuse site. The Government's website www.thinkuknow. co.uk is fine but when it was first set up if you typed 'you' instead of putting 'u' in the website address, then you were taken to an adult content website. Again, look at what you get from their website address: 'think u know' becomes Think UK Now!

- A small company that supplies custom made writing pens has a high street shop (in the USA) named Pen Island. This is not a problem when seen on the sign above the shop; however, when the words run together and are written as a *single word* for the web address, the innocent name becomes something quite different.

Other examples have included:

- www.choosespain.com (Choose Spain)

- www.powergenitalia.com (Powergen Italia)

- www.expertsexchange.com (Experts Exchange)

- www.msexchange.org (MS Exchange). Actually anything that uses the word exchange is going to be a problem with a plural in front of it; it may even make the same visual impact without, since our eyes and brain collude to do funny things.

The moral? Always check out your choice of URL before securing the domain name. You may find an anomaly yourself but as you are so closely attached to the project you may not see what is obvious to someone who is new to the name. It pays to carry out some simple research: write the website address out on some paper, using all lower case as it will appear on the internet and then show it to a number of people and ask them what they see.

The head code and meta names or tags

Now we get into the source code of the site. The first rule when dealing with the source code, particularly if you are not of a technical persuasion, is DON'T PANIC – it is not anywhere near as complicated as it looks.

The second rule is that you will need to use your judgement in your particular situation concerning what you put into your meta names. There is never 'the best way' and no 'right answer'. The only conclusive answer I can ever give to a question concerning metadata is that "it depends". So much so, that I have a small sign that I can hold up to save me saying, "It depends" too often – and to help make the point clearly. (This sounds a bit strange – even to me – when written down, but believe me it is very effective in my seminars; when I have held it up for the fifth time, the delegates get the idea very clearly.)

We can access the source code as earlier (the same as in Chapter 5, What Are Your Competitors Doing?). If you are using Microsoft Internet Explorer version 6 or 7, while looking at the website, position the pointer or cursor in a blank, plain or empty area of the page and right click the mouse. You should see a pop-up dialogue box. Half way down the list, look for the words 'View Source'. Click on this and a window should open displaying the code that makes up the web page you are viewing. (This will probably launch Notepad or some other text viewing application.) Alternatively, you will find 'Source' as a choice in the view menu in many browsers.

We are only interested at this stage in one part of the code. This is easy to find as it is usually at the top of the page. Look for the section defined by the following parameters <head> </head>. This indicates a section of the code that is not normally seen by the user of the site. Its function is to provide instructions for the browser, search engines and other software. Among other things, it contains the meta names (also referred to as meta tags) that contain the details that we (and the search engines) are interested in.

These meta names are used by search engines to catalogue the site, enabling them to list the page in results of searches for the information that is in the meta names. We are basically trying to position information so that the automatic cataloguing process carried out by the search engine software shows the website most accurately and to best advantage. Not all websites contain this information, or they may not be included or organized to the best advantage of the business. If so, the search engines will draw their cataloguing information from other places or pages of the site, and, as this process is automatic, mistakes will be made and your website rating (how high it appears in the listing for a given search) will suffer. It might appear in the wrong search results and make your website less useful or less relevant to the searcher.

It is worth noting that, although they are correctly termed meta names, many people refer to them as meta tags and, when they are discussed individually, the most common way is to refer (as I do in the details below) to the 'description tag', or the 'keywords tag' etc.

If we look at the source code of a web page, as a minimum you should find the title and the following meta names in the head section of the page:

```
<head>
<title>your page title in here</title>
<Meta name="Description" content="Your page description in here">
<Meta name="Keywords" content="Your page keywords in here">
</head>
```

More likely when you look at it, there will be lots of other details present so you will need visually to extract the bits you are looking for.

There are various meta names other than description and keywords, some of which contribute instructions for the search engines; others are relevant to browsers and may affect the display of the site on the user's screen. We will only be dealing with a few of the meta names as below:

```
<head>
<title>your webpage details</title>
<Meta name="Description" content="your webpage details here">
<Meta name="Keywords" content="your webpage details here">
<Meta name="Distribution" content="your webpage details here">
<Meta name="Rating" content="your webpage details here">
<Meta name="Googlebot" content="your webpage details here">
<Meta name="Revisit-After" content="your webpage details here">
<Meta name="Robots" content="your webpage details here">
</head>
```

The head code should be written individually for each page in the site and while it may sometimes be the same as another page – there are usually some instructions which remain constant in every page – what is important is that it accurately reflects the content of that page.

The page title
```
<title> your webpage details </title/>
```
This is the title of the web page and the only one of the meta names that is visible to users when they are browsing your website. Whilst you may never have noticed it or never look at it on screen, where it appears in the title bar of the browser window it is an important part of the optimization process.

It appears as the first line of the search results. In addition, if users should decide to save the page to their favourites (or bookmark the page), it becomes the automatic reference or title in the favourites list. Since many website users do not know that they can change the entry in favourites (or do not know how to), this becomes crucial for being noticed at a later date when users return to their favourites.

So the title is probably the first thing that potential customers will read about your web page or business. Therefore the objective is to write a page title that contains the optimized keywords and phrases whilst still making sense to the readers. Like everything it seems, this is filled with compromise. Remember it also has to make the website stand out when they next look it up in their favourites or bookmark list. So make it plain and simple, make it contain keywords and ensure that it makes sense when read in isolation, out of context, or if just the first bit is visible.

Search engines will display about 65 characters of the title in their results listings, this includes spaces. It is important to use them all to good advantage; employing only a few is a waste and reduces the effective optimization level of the page. How many characters display in the title bar is dependent on the resolution of the user's monitor or screen and how the particular screen is set-up. In addition, some recent versions of browsers such as IE7 use something called tabbed browsing. This means that the title might be displayed in a small tab (that gets smaller as more of them are opened). See Fig. 11. Even though when users click on the tab the full title now shows in the title bar, it is even more important that the keywords are at the beginning and the first part of the title makes sense.

I would not normally include the company name in the page title, although there are exceptions to this. If the company name is not in the website address, then it can be prudent to include it, and if this is the home page to position it at the beginning. Even though when the page is displayed it would be reasonable to assume that the company name is clearly

Fig. 11 Tabbed browsing.

shown on the page itself – in the logo or other page information – when the title is seen in the favourites or bookmarks list or in a tab that is not the currently viewed window (in IE7 etc.), then the company name is not visible. The other reason for including your company name in the title of the home page (if it is not in your website address or URL) is so that it will enjoy high listings for users searching on the company name as opposed to other keywords.

The description tag

The first thing to note is that the description tag describes the content of the page, not the site. This is not a place to put company ethics, principles or mottos. It is not a place for advertising speak, fluff or waffle. The description must be subjective, must make sense, be relevant to the specific content of the page and must give the searcher a reason for clicking on the link. In search results the description appears below the title; so this is also information that a searcher may read before deciding to click on the link to the web page.

Of course, many users do not read the description fully or

even give it more than a cursory glance. With the advent of broadband it can seem – to users – to be just as quick to go to the site itself, to see if it is what they are looking for and if not click on the back button returning to click on the next link in the search results. User testing and eye-tracking research demonstrates that this is the most common behaviour in users. This means that keyword inclusion and positioning is even more important.

The internet is now the first place that people look for contact details or a telephone number. It is easier to look in a search engine than in a telephone directory. (It is also cheaper than using a directory enquiry service.) Including the telephone number in the description can save the user time and help to make the visual connection: numbers are easily spotted as they stand out visually. As this is the type of keyword they are looking for, users may spot your telephone number, even though it might not actually be the one they are looking for. As it is available, they contact your company (instead of your competitor) simply because it is easier and quicker.

This assumes, of course, that the objective of your website is to encourage enquiries and contact. Conversely, if you are not set up to deal with telephone enquiries, do not include your telephone number in the description (although it is important that it is somewhere in the website for the purposes of credibility if nothing else).

The description tag is not limited to 150 words, but only the first 146 will be displayed followed by . . . to indicate there is more. (This applies to Google, but may vary in other search engines.)

If there is no description tag (or it doesn't contain any details), the search engine may either leave a space where the description should be or it may lift the first 150 characters it finds on the web page and insert them into the description field in the results page. This is not always a good solution (for your business). So ensure that you complete the

description tag and that it makes the best sense for your target
website users, your customers and your business.

The keywords tag

A few years ago, Google stopped using the keywords tags;
this practice was followed by the rest of the main search
engines. This has resulted in many (some heated) discussions
on and off the internet on the subject of the keywords section
in the head of web pages, with many people in the SEO
industry saying that you should leave them out. However,
including the keywords is not detrimental to search engine
results; and there are incidences where the keywords tag is
used. Internal searches (where a search is carried out within
the website) will utilize keywords and there may be other
services that do this now or in the future.

The keywords should be prioritized in order of importance
and separated with a comma and a space. Limit the list to
about 25 words or phrases. As with other elements, each page
should have a separate list specific to the contents of the
page.

Your keyword tag should look something like this:
<Meta name="Keywords" content="wordorphrase1,
wordorphrase2, complete this">

Other meta names include:

Distribution tag

The internet is accessible around the world so you have the
opportunity to sell to all points of the globe. From Sheffield to
Singapore anyone who is looking for the products you sell can
buy from you if they find your website.

The distribution tag indicates to the search engines
which countries the site should be displayed in, if a search
local to that country is carried out for your keywords or
phrases.

Global, Europe and United Kingdom are common meta names content for the distribution tag and should be used according to your target customers' location.

For a company trading only in the UK, the tag would look like this:

`<Meta name="Distribution" content="United Kingdom">`

Rating tag

There are two forms of rating:

- *General* which covers all forms of document.

- *Adult* is used if the web page contains content of an adult nature. This instructs browsers that this web page has adult content and is used to activate any parental controls and not allow access to the page.

The rating tag looks like this:

`<Meta name="Rating" content="General">`

The next three tags give the search engines instructions on how their software – robots and spiders – should behave with regard to your website. You would normally expect these tags to be the same on every page.

Googlebot tag

Every second of every hour of every day, small programs access web pages everywhere recording information and sending it back to the vast database of Google (and other search engines). These software programs are called bots, robot or spiders and they have one objective – to collect information. The Google robot is called Googlebot and to ensure that you get listed in the Google database it is worth putting a special instruction to this robot.

If you look at your website statistics, you may be able to see

Search engine name	Robot name
All the web	FAST-WebCrawler
Alta vista	Scooter/Scooter2/Mercator
Google	Googlebot
Infoseek	UltraSeek Infoseek Sidewinder
Lycos	Lycos_Spider_(T-REX)
Mirago	HenryTheMiragoRobot
MSN	MSNBOT/0.1
Teoma	Teoma_agent1
Yahoo/Inktomi	Slurp

Table 5

the robots visiting your website. The main search engine robots are shown in Table 5.

The instruction you give to the Googlebot in this tag is whether you want it to register the information in the web page. Now you might think, "Isn't that the purpose of the site to be registered and get noticed?" For general pages this is true and the tag would read 'All' as below.

<Meta name="Googlebot" content="all">

There are some specific cases where having a page registered would not be appropriate. The news sites are in this range as they can change not by the day or week but by the minute or hour. This means that by the time the search engine registers the page it may have changed a number of times. For this reason, it would not be appropriate for Google to cache (or save information from a given point in time) in their database. In this case, the Googlebot instruction would be 'no follow no cache'.

Revisit tag

It used to be necessary to re-register your website with the search engines every four weeks, but the inclusion of the revisit tag helps to avoid this time consuming activity. This tag instructs the robots to revisit the page after a specified period of time to look for changes.

The period is relative to how often you make changes to the website. For example, if you sell houses or second hand cars and your website changes daily, you might want your site revisited after one day.

If you have a website that is not updated often, the normal period for revisiting would be 28 days. Don't be tempted to reduce the period unless you really do make updates on that basis. Google robots will revisit your site and it they find no changes time after time, the search engine will consider your site to be static and your rating will reduce (meaning that you get a lower position in the listing as a result).

Meta name="Revisit-After" content="28 days">

Robots tag

On each of your pages there will be links to other parts of your site. It is important to instruct the robot to connect to the other parts of your site by following the links both in your navigation and through your text.

The robots will also follow links that go out of your website to other sites. This is why it is beneficial if someone links to your website; the robots visiting their site will follow links to your site. If their site is rated highly and links to your site, your site's rating will be improved.

The instruction for this is 'index, follow'. This means follow all the links from the index page (the default filename for the home page).

<Meta name="Robots"content="index, follow">

Of course, if all this is just too techie for you, then talk to your web developers; they should be dealing with this stuff every day. Also, now you know a little more about it, you will be able to understand more of what they are on about.

Keywords in the website content

The last element that we need to address is the text content of the web pages. The heading text and the first sentence of the first paragraph are particularly important.

The sooner the search engines find keywords and phrases on the page, the better. Of course, as mentioned earlier, you cannot use a particular keyword too often. Search engines also increase the rating on words that are highlighted in bold. But a word of warning: do not take this as an opportunity to make all your text bold. It will not improve your rating and will make your text very hard for your users to read.

In addition, when users search on a particular keyword in a search engine, it makes logical sense that when they arrive at your website they will also be looking for that search term. So ensure that your keywords are in the text content, are used as headings and, in particular, (as mentioned earlier) they are used as the first words of the first sentences of the paragraphs. This makes them stand out to most website users who instead of reading every word will scan the page looking for keywords.

Alt text

Alt text is used to provide a text alternative for images. This is required for your website to comply with the Disability Discrimination Act 1995. It is also an opportunity for including keywords without exceeding reasonable limits for the number of keywords on a page.

The most important thing to remember about writing the meta names for your website is that there is no hard and fast rule about what to say and where to include them. To sum it up, 'it depends'. The other important point is that once you have written them, you need to experiment, observe and track your website results so that you can assess their effectiveness. Once they are written, they should not be considered as set in stone but as a flexible inclusion in your website that you will change from time to time to respond to changes in your business and your market.

8

COMMUNICATING WITH YOUR WEB DESIGNERS OR DEVELOPERS

Imagine taking a seat in a restaurant and, without knowing what kind of restaurant it is, or without so much as a glance at the menu, calling a waiter over to serve you. "I want a meal," you say. "What can I get you?" asks the waiter. "Food, bring me some food, I'm hungry, I need a meal and I've been told this is a good place," you respond. "What sort of meal do you want?" asks the waiter. "Are you very hungry, would you like three courses or would you like a light snack?" "I don't know, this is a restaurant isn't it, you're the experts, you tell me," you demand.

So, with no concern for whether you might have specific requirements that have not been communicated to the waiter, you abdicate every decision to the restaurant. Even the most complex menu would be unlikely to produce this response in the most inexperienced of restaurant-goers. Furthermore, I wonder what would be the reaction from a vegetarian who was faced with a steak in response to his unspecified order, or the diabetic who was brought the most sugary of desserts.

Now, if you are very lucky, or the waiter happens to be tele-pathic, you might get a meal that suits your requirements. You can be sure you will get a meal, but will it fulfil your specific needs? Will it be to your taste? Will it be just right to satisfy your level of hunger? Will your budget accommodate it? Will it take into account your personal idiosyncrasies? (My wife insists on having sauces served separate to her food; if the food arrives 'swimming' – as she puts it – it always gets sent back.)

It is much more likely that a meal will indeed arrive, but it will be not quite what you were hoping for. After all, we have acknowledged that we cannot expect the waiter to be telepathic. However, this is often the plight of web designers.

I discussed in Chapter 2, Setting Objectives for Your Website, how important it is that you are clear on what you want to achieve with your website and how it will serve your business.

We surveyed many web design companies; without fail, they *all* reported that every so often (or even very often) the initial web design meeting goes something like this:

New client: "Hi, um, I need a website and my friend/colleague/brother-in-law/bloke I met in a queue at the supermarket said that you were good."

Web designer: "OK, fine, what is the website for?"

New client: "Well it is for me" (sounds slightly confused)

Web designer: "I mean is it for your business, or . . . ?"

New client: "Oh yes, it is for my business."

Web designer: "And what type of business are you in?" (Realizing by now that information is going to have to be dragged, kicking and screaming out of this one.)

New client: "Well, the business is new and we haven't quite decided exactly what type/range/offering of ready-meals/car spares/garden landscaping we are going to be doing yet."

Web designer: "OK, so what is the purpose of the website, and what do you want it to do? What sort of features and functionality do you require?"

New client (completely lost): "What do you mean? I need a website, can you make me one?"

Web designer: "Yes of course, but I need to know what you want."

New client: "Well you're the web designer, you're the expert, you tell me!"

Web designer (trying not to get exasperated): "OK, let's start from the beginning."

New client: "What do you mean . . . oh and how much is this going to cost me?" (Sounding more confused/agitated/by the minute.)

Web designer: "Well that obviously depends on what you want."

New client: "I want a website . . . you must be able to give me some idea of how much it will cost."

. . . and so on it goes.

Sound familiar at all? You would never go into a restaurant and demand that the waiter brought you a meal without making some choices, including probably having some idea of what kind of meal you require before you make your choice of restaurant and walk in through the door.

Yet every single web designer I have spoken to over the last ten years has had some kind of experience like the above. What's more worrying, it doesn't seem to be getting any better.

Sometimes it can be the web designers who create this situation. They can be so keen to obtain the work in what is now a highly competitive market that sometimes they don't ask the right questions or sometimes they don't know the right questions to ask.

The moral? If the web designer or developer you speak to doesn't require you to provide detail about your objectives and your business (i.e. a web design brief of any kind), go elsewhere.

The website design brief
The website design brief is the document that guides the web designers and developers. It is the statement of who you and your business are, what you perceive you need, who you are

aiming at, what you hope the website will do, what the parameters are, what the designers are to do. Simply handing the responsibility for the website over to the developer is highly unlikely to result in the best return on your investment.

It is probably the most often referred-to document in the whole web design and development process. The designers or development team cannot be expected to be telepathic. They can only work from the information they are given, and in this case the majority of it is, or should be, recorded in the design brief.

We surveyed 57 web development companies and looked at hundreds of web design brief documents. While everyone does it slightly differently (just as there are dozens of ways to cook eggs), there were many things common to them all. Below, we will cover all the crucial elements that need to be included, as well as mentioning some of the other things that I think are important.

Remember that a book of this type is a broad guide and is never going to be able to cover something like this in a level of detail that would include every possible situation or desired outcome. That said, a book that did would probably be so complicated, difficult to read, or downright boring, that you wouldn't be reading it.

First things first. There are a few things you need to keep in your head as you prepare this document.

- **This document needs to be a clear, concise, structured communication.** Put really simply, unless you can communicate what you want, you cannot possibly hope to get it. The person who knows more about your business than anyone else is you. Do not expect a web developer to know the 'who', 'what', 'why' and 'where' of your business.

- **You are preparing this document because you are contracting someone outside your business.** At least it should be someone outside your business unless your company is big enough to have a design department. If you haven't, you should definitely be looking at someone outside your business. (For more information on this, see Chapter 9, Finding a Web Design Company.)

- **Be aware that your web designers don't necessarily know anything about your business or industry.** It is easy inadvertently to use language or jargon from your industry that your web designers may not necessarily understand.

  It is reasonable to expect the designers to carry out research and gain some understanding of your industry, but this would be from a visual communication, branding or customer perception point of view, not every little bit of detail that you have gained from your years of involvement.

  To get a clearer image of this, ask yourself the following. How long have you been in your industry? How long did it take you to get to grips with the language, technical terms, and esoteric methods of how your business or industry works? I bet it wasn't measured in hours or even days. Now consider the overall scale of your web development project. Is there really time for your web designers to get to know your industry properly?

  Your web designers are likely to encounter different types of businesses and industries all the time and, while the more experienced designers may have some familiarity with yours, it is your responsibility to ensure they are fully informed.

- **Don't take knowledge or anything else for granted**. If you have a piece of information that you are unsure as to whether you need to include it or leave it out, then include it.

  I have lost count of the number of times I have discussed what is deemed to be an unsuccessful website (the lack of success being blamed on the designers or developers) and then discovered that a crucial piece of information (such as the company merging with another or changing its name to appeal to a different market, a new product range being imminent or an existing one being cancelled) was withheld from the design team because it was not considered to be important or relevant (or more commonly 'any of their business to know').

Developing a website design brief
So what do we need to include?

This section is split into three parts:

- The **'essentials'** – the information that you cannot afford to leave out.

- The **'desirables'** – which include subsidiary information that will help your designers to do a good job and help them pretend they are telepathic after all.

- And, the **'it might be a good idea to mention**ables**'** which includes the stuff that you think the design team might not necessarily need, but it is better to include than not.

THE 'ESSENTIALS'
A profile of your business
The only person who can really know about your business is you. The designers will require specific information (that follows below) but still need to hear your own view of your business. Include a succinct description of your company covering:

- Its history, how and why it began.

- Its mission – what the company is in business to do, or be the best at or achieve or whatever.

- Its vision – where it is going. Is there a planned exit point or strategy?

- Its current position – where it is now, the number of employees, turnover, etc.

- Its products and/or services.

Company image and/or product brands
Any existing or established company image or product brand imagery that is in current or future planned use must be supplied. This is so that the designers can – to the best of their ability within the constraints placed on them – support and not conflict with how your company is currently perceived by its customers.
   This would include (but is not limited to):

- Existing logos or logotype (a logo made up of letterforms).

- A copy of your business stationery: letterheads, business cards, etc.

- Any brochures, flyers or leaflets that you distribute.

- Posters, billboards.

- Newspaper or magazine adverts.

- TV and even radio advertising. (Even though you might think that there are no pictures on the radio, the advert will be conveying some impression to the listener, brand positioning or similar.)

- A copy of, or links to, any existing online presence: websites, directory entries, yellow pages ads, any online advertisements, membership organizations which may have reference to your business on their website. (In Chapter 5, What Are Your Competitors Doing?, there are instructions on how to use Google to find all the references to your business that are currently in their database. This can help you to find entries that you may have forgotten about.)

Even if you are commissioning a new corporate image or brand identity along with this website project, you still need to supply information on where you are now.

Future plans
This would be the place to include details of any existing plans or possibilities for the development of the business. This might be plans to change the name, to merge with or acquire other businesses, restructuring, any new products or services, if you are planning to move or open new or additional offices or facilities, etc. Don't forget to include any plans to commission new brand or corporate imagery, especially if from another company.

Objectives of the website
Identify the main reason for having a website as well as any secondary objectives. We covered this in some detail in Chapter 2 and you should have also revisited the objectives when prompted. If you have gone through the book chapter by chapter you should now be able to define your website objectives clearly.

Website content
In a general sense, websites can be thought of as containing two things: structure and content. The structure consists of the pages and how they inter-relate, the navigation system and hyperlinks between the pages and out of the website. The content consists of the text and images (and video or whatever else) contained on the pages. So when we refer to content, we are usually referring to text and images.

It is the content that anyone visits the website for. The structure is crucial, but, to the user, should not really be visible or any kind of an issue. (If it is, then it is not very well designed.)

You need to list the main content elements that you or your customers want to see in the site. Providing a sample will not only allow the designers to judge the type and tone of the content, but also indicate as to whether (in their opinion) you are able to provide these to a sufficient standard. In an ideal world, you (or your web developer on your behalf) would contract a copywriter to produce the text content, and a photographer and/or graphic designer or graphic artist to produce the images. The web designers or development company may well offer some of these services, some may be included, but expect to be charged.

You should not kid yourself that you can save money by writing the text copy yourself or taking photographs of your product offerings if you are really not up to the job. You wouldn't offer to cater for your favourite niece's wedding if you never made more than beans on toast on a regular basis. The same applies here. If you take photos on holiday and at family occasions, and the most writing you do is the occasional report or thank you letter, then leave it to the professionals. We have a mantra in our consultancy practice, 'Be an expert, use an expert'. You may have seen the excellent television advert for BT featuring Gordon Ramsey fitting his own computer system while the kitchen is on fire and disaster reigns in the background[1]. Every time you think 'I could do that (and save some money)', remember Gordon Ramsay tightening a screw with a huge kitchen knife.

Target market
Briefly describe your traditional or existing market (customers) and identify who the website will be targeting (if it's not the same thing).

If you are currently in, or are planning to target, a Business to Consumer (B2C) market, your brief should include some

---

1. At the time of writing, a video of this advert could be viewed online (for free) at http://www.tellyads.com/show_movie.php?filename=TA3339.

detail and demographic information, who your customers are, what age group, where they live, what kind of income they may have or what their spending power might be, if they are married, if they have children, what other kinds of products they buy, etc.

If you are operating in a Business to Business (B2B) market, then information on the size of the company/number of employees/turnover, etc. of the businesses that currently buy from you, the type of industry they are in, and a brief list of current or potential customers including web addresses might prove useful.

In Chapter 4, Who is the Website for Anyway?, I discussed targeting customers in some detail; this will help you ensure that you provide suitable information to the designers.

The competition
This is information about the industry in which you operate: who your main competitors are; also, who the main players in your industry are. A short list, together with web addresses, will help the designers to get a feel for the industry and how it portrays itself to its market.

How is your business differentiated from your competitors? Why do they buy from you instead of them? Do you have any specific selling points that could be described as unique (USP), social (SSP) or emotional (ESP)? These are discussed in some detail in Chapter 5, What Are Your Competitors Doing?

Scope
This is about the scope of the project and what exactly you are expecting the design company to do (or not do).

For example:

• Do you want them to provide you with a domain name, email addresses and hosting for your website? Or do you already have a domain name set up? Perhaps there is a website currently on that domain name that the new one will be replacing.

- Do they have to work with your existing website hosting company? (Many designers are not happy or even willing to do this. It tends to cause them lots of problems and extra work that they cannot charge for and can easily eat up the small amount of profit they will make on a project.)

- How often do you want to update the content? Will you want to do this yourself using some kind of content management system?

- Is the website going to sell or advertise a large selection of stock which will require a database developed in order to manage this?

- Will you be providing the content and images (see content section above)?

- Will you need it to integrate with other software or systems that you currently use?

Scale

Also describe the scale of the project. Either estimate roughly how many pages you expect to be in the site or the number of individual products or services it will cover. The figures can be very general since a few pages more or less will rarely alter the cost or timing of the project.

Project constraints

You need to be clear in your plans and have deadlines set for milestones in the project. These can include:

- Appointing a web design/development team.

- Project start date.

- Design 'roughs' for initial approval.

- Site build – structure and navigation, databases, etc.

- Supply of content.

- Testing.

- Site to go live.

You also need a rough idea of the budget, bearing in mind that the more you ask for, the more it will cost.

Point of contact
Be sure to provide the name, phone number and email address of *one* person who the designers can approach with any questions. Ideally this person will be someone who can either make decisions or action their requests and will be their point of contact throughout the work.

THE 'DESIRABLES'
Maybe you have seen something on a website that you like and would like to include. Before you ask for this, ensure that it will serve your objectives in some way or provide added value or ease of use for your customers.

Examples of things that satisfy this might include calculators of any kind such as mortgage repayments calculators or currency conversion tools. (But only if they use current information sourced from an expert information site. Inaccurate figures are worse than none at all.) Of course, these things cost money and it can be just as effective simply to link to the correct page in another site such as www.xe.com which has a free currency converter tool on the home page.

Other useful tools or facilities include order tracking. This works so that once you have dispatched the goods, customers can track where their delivery is at any given point in time. However, unless you represent a multinational company, it is unlikely that you could afford this. In any case, there is no need since most of the large haulage, logistics and delivery companies provide this service. You simply have to set up a process to inform customers of the appropriate order code or tracking number, and provide instructions and links for them to be able to get to the right place easily. Amazon uses this technique.

As you can see from the above examples, many 'desirables' are not actually needed and you can often save money with a workaround or simply by linking to somewhere that the service is available already.

My colleague, who ran a web design company for over ten years, gave me a list of some of the most commonly requested 'desirables'.

They include:

- Welcome or intro pages, or some kind of welcome text, graphic or animation.

- Websites built using Flash, so that they look and behave differently from most websites.

- Pop-up windows or other elements that appear on the screen unannounced prompting action of some kind (buy now!).

- Screen elements such as scroll bars that have been redesigned so that they don't really look like scroll bars and look like something else or are themed (such as scroll bars that look like rope for a site in the yachting industry – yes really, I didn't make that up).

- Music that plays automatically when the site or a page is launched or opened (and not when it is a sample of music available for sale or download).

- Pictures of the company owner, managing director or chief executive (and their families) on the home page.

As regards the list opposite, you shouldn't include any of them so don't even think about it! Most of the items are in the results of our extended research of the things that people most hate about websites. For more information on this, see Chapter 1, What is Wrong with the Current Website?

So the word of warning on 'desirables': proceed with caution on what you ask for. No-one could blame a web design or development company for supplying you with something that you ask for. It is not their job to ensure the success of your business. It is their job to produce the website you specify. If you are replacing an existing website, the last position you want to find yourself in is back at the beginning.

THE 'IT MIGHT BE A GOOD IDEA TO MENTIONABLES'

This is where you include anything that you may not really consider to be relevant. Hopefully you will take the advice mentioned earlier in this chapter and include it rather than leave it out.

The most commonly missed out information is to do with future plans. If you have decided or are only at the discussion stage, let the designers know. This may be things that are directly to do with the website (for example, you intend that next year you will start selling online) or that seem unrelated to it (for example, the business is going to merge with another and acquire their successful brands).

One example stands out in my mind where a company stated in the *target market* section, that all their customers were in the UK. In the *objectives of the website* they had stated that they might want to use the website to enhance business opportunities *either* to Europe or the USA. In the *future plans* section, there was no mention of any of this.

This might seem like a reasonable goal, to expand a UK only business into European countries *or* to the USA, and to the business this is completely reasonable. But consider this prospect from a web developer's viewpoint. If their client requires a website for Europe, immediately consideration is needed to make provision for other European languages, the translation and cultural issues and how this will be set up and be managed. For the USA, languages are not a problem as such, but the website content should take into account UK/USA English usage differences. There are also issues relating to optimization that require consideration if you are intending to target another country.

This is only one small point, and the tip of the iceberg. There are a myriad of cultural and regional legislative issues to be aware of. If the website is for the UK only, there is no need for any of this to be of concern. Not considering or informing the designers of these kinds of decisions can result in a lot of extra expenditure in the future. Even though the term 'future proof'[2] is an oxymoron (a contradiction in a phrase) you should make the best effort you can to consider what the future is likely to hold and plan for it.

You need to be clear on your future plans. If you contract someone to fit a new bathroom in your house, you have to tell them where the individual items are going to be positioned. You can't say "Maybe the bath will go there but I haven't decided yet," when the builders are standing in your house with a spanner in one hand.

Please ensure that you have not included the designers' nightmare: the two statements that either clearly or more subtly contradict each other. Or worse where a question remains that affects every part of the project and, without a clear answer, they find themselves in a position where they cannot begin.

2.. How can something be 'future proof' if you cannot see the future?   If you had a time machine then you would not need a website as you could bet on the horses and make far more money!

And finally . . .

When you have done all of this, go back and review it. In particular, check that you haven't missed anything out. Why not ask a colleague or employee to read it through? It is amazing the tiny things that are obvious but that become invisible when you get close to something.

Be clear in your mind that when you commission a website for your business, you are contracting something that can have an effect on every part of how you operate and which can potentially hold the key to your future failure or success.

Free download

A template for completing the website design brief in the form of a Word document is available for download free of charge from our website. This URL will take you directly to the document:

www.businessforbusiness.co.uk/websitedesignbrief.htm

9

FINDING A WEB DESIGN COMPANY

"Find a web developer?" I can hear you saying, "I don't need to find a web developer, I am going to build the website myself, that's why I am reading this book."

In my many years' experience of advising small businesses this is symptomatic of one of the most common stumbling blocks that contribute to the lack of success of a small business.

It's nothing to do with the internet. It is the apparent belief that you can do everything yourself. I hear it all the time: "Why would I spend good money paying someone to: do my book-keeping/clean the office/develop a website?" And so your expenses receipts for the last year overflow from the bottom drawer of your desk; you stop noticing the crumbs in the carpet on your office floor and your website damages your business day-in-day-out. All because you thought you could do it yourself. In truth, you either don't have the skills or, if you do, you don't have the time.

Do you really have the skills?
If you are really determined to build your own website, take a look at the list below as a checklist of skills (bearing in mind

that, if the project is large, this checklist might apply to a team). Are you able to:

- Apply prior experience to establish the viable objective for the website within the budget and desired timescale?

- Carry out secondary research in your industry to identify competitors' online strategies without previous bias ("I know all about them")?

- Develop or interpret your business's or product's brand identity, value and differentiation in a way that is appropriate to the medium?

- Design a usable, accessible screen layout, suitable for multiple screen resolutions and browsers?

- Create a logical information architecture suitable for your specific data requirement, in a hierarchical structure taking into account the greater than 60 per cent chance of multiple entry points?

- Develop an intuitive navigation system that serves the above structure effectively, while ensuring that the website users will be able adequately to have a sense of 'where they are and where they have already been'?

- Construct the website using suitable software to create screen graphics, HTML page construction and any supplementary code required to meet the objectives?

- Ensure that the site is devoid of internal errors and test against minimum usability and accessibility criteria?

- Optimize the website for search engines, inserting the appropriate meta names and keywords?

Not forgetting, of course, to apply the knowledge and experience that designers would (or should) have of:

- Branding, colour theory and visual communication.

- Design principles that might apply to this situation:
    - Affordance; confirmation, forgiveness and constraint.
    - Progressive disclosure and layering.
    - Mapping and mental models.
    - Fitt's law.
    - And a whole variety of others too numerous to mention here . . .

- Online user behaviour, eye-tracking research, website conventions.

I could go on . . .

There is a lot of jargon in the above lists, and I certainly don't expect you to understand what all of it means. Jargon is something I usually avoid at all costs. However, I have left it in here to help make the point that this is a profession all of its own, hopefully occupied by professionals.

There are two items in the first list that this book is meant to assist with, specifically:

- Optimize the website for search engines, inserting the appropriate meta names and keywords.

- Ensure that the site is devoid of internal errors and test against minimum usability and accessibility criteria. Translated, this means: make sure that it works and does the job it is supposed to do; is easy to use for everyone regardless of ability or disability.

But the rest of it is another matter. In any case, there is no book on the market that can make anyone a designer or web developer just by reading it, even if he or she had a brain the size of a planet.

If the website is a larger project – maybe you want other functionality such as a catalogue and shopping cart – you will need to be skilled at database development and online implementation, SQL programming, JavaScript and so on. To accommodate your objectives or criteria, the programming might require a technical team of software developers. Even setting up a brochure website would require the developer to have a general understanding of the complexity of Hyper Text Mark up language (HTML) code. (For when something in the most basic website goes wrong or you need to access the code to tweak the metadata or to accommodate alternative browser technology – assuming you knew that you needed to – and your HTML generating software doesn't have an option in a dialog box for it, not that you were looking for it . . . I hope that soon I can rest my case on this.)

Then there are the legal requirements of Accessibility. "I don't need to worry about that," you might be thinking. "People with disabilities are not my target customer or they represent a very small percentage."

It has been estimated that something like a third of the people in the UK have some sort of physical or mental difficulty that makes their life and their activities online a little or a lot harder. Do you intend to reject one third of the population as potential customers? Even if the moral issues or the profit angle one didn't get to you, as mentioned in Chapter 1, What is Wrong with the current Website?, it is a legal requirement.

Never underestimate that your website – like it or not – is your public statement of who you are and what you do. It is the place where people go to find out about you, and you have about two minutes maximum to make the right impression, and only 10 seconds or so to get people to stay after their first arrival. So it's not so easy now you come to think of it. Make no mistake, a poor website will at best not help you at all (so you will have wasted your time) and at worst do daily damage that you are not even aware of – it is not possible to measure the sales or leads that you didn't get.

Be an expert, use an expert

So once you've thought about the skills that you will need, do you have the time to be messing about trying to learn something that you don't know how to do when you should really be getting on with what you do, your business? It is hard to estimate the opportunity cost (the potential income that you might have made if you weren't busy trying to set up your own website) and the danger of becoming distracted and taking your eye off the ball (of your business activities).

You may well think it is not going to take very long to set up a little website, but in order to do your business justice, it just is not possible to learn all the skills required in a few weeks that normally take years to master. People don't go to university for three or four years to learn something that you can figure out for yourself in a few days. Ask any designer how long it took to become competent. If he or she is mature and honest the answer will probably be, "About ten years or so after graduating," and that the learning never stops.

It has often been said that the secret of success is 'surrounding yourself with clever or successful people'. In a small business or, in particular, in a sole-trader business, this is not an option. By definition, there are not many people, so you can only get this by buying it in, by contracting an expert.

The moral of the story is if you want to be successful: be an expert; use an expert. When it comes to any kind of technology – even if you work at it more than full-time, or are virtually obsessed with it – you can't learn it all. And anyway by the time you have learnt it, it will have changed.

So I cannot recommend strongly enough that unless you already have the skills (which would mean that you are working in or have experience in a related industry, e.g. you are a graphic designer and your wife is a programmer), you should contract the work to an expert.

What is design anyway?
An insight into what the industry does

Whichever way you look at it, web design has to be considered the confluence or meeting point of two distinct disciplines: design and technology. While design was influenced by technology as a tool for production or creativity before the inception of the web, never previously was technology the medium for design.

In the early days of web design (the 1990s), many of those who explored and adopted this new medium evolved out of digital graphic design. At the time, there were widespread predictions that the web would be the death of print (i.e. the magazine and publishing industry), as well as the end of brochures and marketing literature (the bread-and-butter work of many graphic designers). Interestingly, this turned out to be more than inaccurate. There are now far more magazines published than before the internet became mainstream.

It is widely understood that there are almost as many definitions of the word design as there are designers. Many say, including Don Norman, in his excellent book *The Design of Everyday Things*, that design is "problem solving within constraints".

In the influential words of ex Royal College of Art teacher Norman Potter, "The designer works with and for other people."[1] As Peter Saville (an influential designer) commented "... as a graphic designer you are not independent; your job is to shape a communication given by another. You may want to articulate your own message, but at that point you're not being a graphic designer."[2]

---

1. Book review of *Design and Art*, edited by Alex Coles, Whitechapel and the MIT press 2007. Quoted by John Stones in *Icon Magazine* p 149, issue 047 May 2007.
2. Peter Saville, 'Documents . . .', Icon Magazine p53, issue 051, Sept 2007.

It's a bit like when singer-songwriters take major roles in films. They then become actors/actresses. They cannot make excuses for their behaviour in their new context, or say that their performance is sub-standard because they needed to express themselves creatively, or say that they did not like the character. They have taken on a specific job and are now on a movie set, as the puppet of the combined string-pulling of the screenwriter and director.

Whichever you prefer, design that serves a business objective is about enabling that business to function better in some way. Whether it is about identity, branding or effective communication, the designers that you select must be equipped to provide you with this.

Where to begin looking

Sourcing a web design or development company is like looking for any other kind of contractor, so your initial approach would be the same as looking for, say, a plumber.

Your first port of call might be the websites of others in your industry, or other types of industries who have the same customers or even your competitors. This may sound a little strange and is something to be approached with caution, although there is logic underpinning this.

If the designers or developers have already worked in your industry, then they already know something about it and will have to some extent researched it.

As an expert in your own industry, you will have the opportunity to gain greater insight into whether the designers have the ability to represent your business to your clients than if you were judging their work in a variety of situations. If they have created other websites to appeal to a specific customer base (e.g. teenagers), they may well specialize in that target and be more successful at it than a more general company. Remembering that the point of all this is to meet your business objectives by communicating effectively to your target customer.

Many years ago I was involved in a new product development from concept to market. When it came to the image and marketing material for the product (this was pre-internet) the client (who was paying the bills) became stuck on the idea of using a particular agency. Their work was exciting; there was great variety and a level of professionalism and confidence that is not often seen unless you are paying 'top-dollar'. They had positioned themselves very well, reassuringly expensive, but not out of reach. Despite my expressed misgivings, the client was determined: the agency was commissioned, the designs and copy were produced.

There was an impressive presentation; they were beautifully crafted, at the same time attractive and dynamic, an altogether inspirational experience. Notably, they met almost all the criteria that had been supplied to them. Just one was missing. They had entirely failed to gain any understanding of the customer. The new product only had one type of customer and they completely failed to understand the nature of the industry, how it functioned, what it currently considered to be appropriate, etc. Instead, the designs looked like something to do with Formula One; the copy sounded like a tourist brochure. An argument ensued about this where the suitability was disputed. To solve this, I initiated some field testing and lo-and-behold the feedback I received from the actual customer was 100 per cent negative. Some of the feedback included: "It looks like something to do with fast cars," "This must be expensive," and "Probably a waste of money." This comment finalized the dispute and a revised version was produced.

If the agency had already created other proposals to appeal to the same customer being targeted in this project, they would have had a level of understanding of what was understood in that industry and a lot of resources (time, money and stress) would have been saved.

Going to those who may have helped your competitors, however, brings with it inherent risks. If you approach someone and they consider there might be a conflict of interest – respect them for that. On the other hand, if a company is very keen and forthcoming with its privileged knowledge, then remember that they are likely to do the same to your business when the next customer comes along.

Home or away?

While most businesses look to contract all kinds of services in their own geographical area, often purely for practical reasons, this may be the one time that it is not necessary as most of the communication can take place by email. In the world of the internet professional, in principle it makes no difference where in the world you are. As a matter of fact, this is one of the reasons for it being such an attractive profession to enter. If, however, you like to have face-to-face contact (or are technologically challenged), this will narrow your options. Of course, if you are working with someone who is just down the road, this can make some things easier, but easier is not always better. Keep your eye on the objective and the outcomes, and how this will be achieved on a practical level.

Recommendation is one of the best options. If someone you know in business tells you that he is really happy with his web design company, that firm might be a good place to start. If, however, someone in the pub tells you that his neighbour's son is a whizz-kid on the computer, then this is definitely one to avoid.

Searching for someone suitable

The traditional route is Yellow Pages, business directories or local business services. Your local business support agency might have lists of recommended or quality assured companies.

Online searching is going to result in millions of results. Searching on Google for 'web designer' returns 132 million; constraining the search by selecting 'UK only' and searching on 'web designer Bristol' still results in over 2 million. Searching on 'web designer small business website Bristol' returns around half a million – get the idea?

However, there is some value in looking at the first few pages of results. If a company is able to get itself in the first few pages in such a highly competitive market, there is some chance that its people know what they are doing. Local online business directories may help to reduce choice a little but cannot necessarily be trusted in terms of quality as there is not usually any kind of accreditation or checking system.

An interesting point to note is that the ones with the best advertising may not necessarily be the best ones for you. It is worth remembering that all that advertising has to be paid for somehow. While it may well represent part of a very successful business model, a lot of expensive advertising relative to the number of clients or a low average project size, may be paid for by cost cutting. This can be achieved in a number of ways including: charging more; doing it quicker; paying their people less; development strategies such as using pre-setup templates. This is never a choice I would recommend: you tend to see that every site they produce looks like every other one, there are often variations but ultimately you end up bending your business to suit the website template, not having a website built to suit your business.

How to narrow down what you find
Whichever way you carry out your searches, you are going to have a big list of potential web designers or development companies.

What is their website like?
The narrowing down process can be started by first taking a look at their site. Bear in mind that this is a website that has been built to profile a design and technology company that is

competing in its own industry. It is important that you are not too swayed by what you see here. It is not necessarily representative of what they might produce for their clients, including you.

Particularly do not be distracted by anything 'clever'. By which I mean things that pop-up on the screen or follow your mouse around, bits of animation or bouncing balls in general. While impressive at first glance, these are often a nightmare to use. You only want any of these things if you can justify how they will help your customers. If you remain impressed despite this, take a look back to Chapter 1, What is Wrong with the Current Website?, for the list of what people most hate about websites.

Probably the most important indicator is: do they appear to care about their own website? The old proverb about cobbler's children[3] often rings true – and I will be the first to admit that there have been times in the past when my own website has been out of date or needed updating with current information; always because I have been giving priority to a client and allocating resources entirely outside rather than inside the business. I would never, of course, recommend that you do this. In order to maintain the longevity and/or growth of a business, some resources must always be allocated to the business, not the clients of the business. All that said, if there are spelling mistakes and broken links in their site then beware; they clearly have no regard for attention to detail and might well be avoided.

What do they offer?
The next step is to assess their suitability on the basis of what they offer.

---

3. A cobbler's children are always down at heel/have no shoes/are the worst shod, depending on where you read it, meaning that you give your clients all your attention and ignore what is happening at home; a busy cobbler will be so busy making shoes for others that there is no time or inclination left at the end of the working day to make or repair the shoes of his children.

What type of websites do they build? What do they say they do? What type of technology do they deal with, and does this concur with your objectives? It depends on whether you need a simple brochure-ware website or are seeking a company that can handle a whole online business venture. Do they deal with online shopping and credit card transactions? If that is what you need, then that is what you are looking for. Do they set up databases, install content management systems, etc?

Whatever your requirements, you are going to be best served by contracting a company that does the type of thing you require regularly.

What level of support can they offer? How quickly can they respond to requests for updates and what if your site goes down for some reason? Do they have technical support if you are going to be managing it yourself? One consideration is the number of people in the web design company. In particular, if your website is going to be mission critical (i.e. your business could fail without it), then what will happen if there is a problem and how will they deal with it?

The crux of this is can they provide what you need? This must be in terms of functionality, suitability for your clients, within your budget and timescale.

Who have they worked for?
What type of customers do they have, does this match your needs? The majority of web design companies will have links to their clients' webpages or their portfolio.

Follow the links to their clients' websites and conduct a brief review. You are trying to identify what type of sites they build and for whom. Is their client base mainly small businesses or larger companies? Do they deal with businesses that mainly function online, or are they concentrating on public sector information websites?

While it is not essential that they are matched to your type of company – and many successful web designers have a wide variety of clients – it makes sense that if a company mainly deals with large public sector websites, and you are a small start-up business who is hoping to employ a few people before the end of the year, then this may not be a good match. (In fact, they may not even be interested in your commission.)

Larger development companies tend to have larger clients and have the turnover and overheads to match. This can mean that a small contract for £1,500 is just not worth their while taking on. At the other end of the scale, a company that normally produces a website of just six or seven pages for under £1,000 may be very willing to take on your big project, but they simply may not have the resources and experience to cope.

What are their clients' websites like?
Looking at the sites they have already produced can give you a good insight into the kind of thing they are doing, or more accurately, have done so far.

Style
You would expect experienced designers to be in a position to interpret your existing company or brand identity (assuming that you have one) or come up with a new visual image if this is a new business or new product offering. All designers develop their own style and, even when this is applied to different projects or interpreted in different ways, you can often identify a style that just 'looks like' a specific designer or design team carried out the work.

Don't consider this to be a negative, it is normal. What is important is whether you like what you see, whether the style appeals to you. More importantly, does it suit your business/brand/product range? Even more importantly, remembering what was discussed in Chapter 4, Who is the Website for Anyway?, will it appeal to your target audience, will they like it, respond to it, buy from it? It is an established design principle that we are attracted to the familiar and that things we find attractive are perceived as easier to use. One way to get a feel for this is to ask some of your existing customers their opinion of the websites your prospective designers have developed.

Woman's work?

Consider the value of employing or contracting female designers if you are targeting a female audience. Most web designers are male, the industry is perceived as being cool and most technology is still male dominated yet most of the purchasing decisions (in a B2C market) are made by women. If you are working in a B2C market, this may be a factor that gives you the edge over the competition.

Seeking references

It is possible to use the information you have already found to seek references before you make contact. This has become common practice and we always recommend that you do this first. Once you have compiled a short list (or a not-so-short list) obtain the contact details of some of their clients. This should – if the websites have been well designed – be easy to find. Phone them. I can hear the voices saying, "I can't do that!" but what do you have to lose? I have never encountered a bad response. If you are honest and straightforward, you are unlikely to encounter a problem. My opening normally goes something like:

"Hi, my name is [your name], and I'm from [your company]. I'm sorry to bother you, but I was looking at your website and I really like it [flattery always creates a little goodwill], I was thinking of approaching the company who designed your site to do mine and I was wondering if you wouldn't mind letting me know what they were like to work with?"

The kind of things you need to know include: were they flexible and easy to get on with?; were they available when the client tried to make contact?; did they answer queries in a straightforward way?; did they deliver on time and on budget (and if not why not)?; were there any contractual issues or disputes? Include any other concerns that you might have. Remember to be careful how you word your questions. It is easy to slip over the line into sounding nosey or as if you are conducting industrial espionage and alienate the person who is helping you for free. The final question should be, "Would you ask them to build another site for you?"

Make a note of the information you get. Once you have talked to half a dozen people you will have no idea who said what about whom. Also remember that what they tell you is *their experience* of that company. They may have a problem with things that don't concern you. Do you ever look at websites with reviews of holiday resorts or hotels? I read one recently that complained bitterly about the lack of facilities and activities for young children at the hotel. As I don't have children, this would not bother me one iota; in fact it is a positive thing as people with young children won't be going as there are no facilities. But it would certainly put off someone who had three children under the age of six.

It is also worth realizing that one of the most common reasons for websites not coming in on budget is because of the lack of preparation by the clients, mainly that they don't know what they want, who it is for, what kind of facilities are required and so on. The main reason for websites not coming in on time is due to delays by the client in providing content.

Shortlist
On the basis of the research you have collected, you now need to shortlist (an actual *short* list this time, maybe maximum of six) and contact the relevant companies. Also make a note of when you contacted them, how quickly they responded, and

what your first or lasting impressions of them were. This is one of the factors that may be the 'straw that broke the camel's back' in the long run – someone who you can never get hold of, or who doesn't answer the phone or doesn't respond to emails for days.

Once you have made contact, arrange meetings with the potential designers. You need to allow something like an hour for each and tell them that when you make the arrangement. Ensure also that you will have sufficient time between the meetings for comfort breaks, to discuss your thoughts (with colleagues) and to make notes. This will take a minimum of 30 minutes. (Don't underestimate this.) This means that you can realistically manage to interview four or maybe five companies in one day; that said, more than three or four and it all starts to become a bit of a blur. Better to spread it over a few days.

It will be beneficial to you if you can arrange for a second or third person to be present at the interview meetings on your behalf. One of your team who may be in a position to provide insight, the person who is going to be responsible for the project or will be their main point of contact should be there. If you are a sole trader, perhaps you can call in a favour from an associate or advisor.

Meetings
Prepare a list of questions. It is much like interviewing for an employee, but differs in that they are going to be functioning outside your organization. Questions need to be centred on meeting your objectives and might include: how long have they been trading, what their background and/or qualifications are, how did they come to be web designers? Do they have any knowledge or experience relative to your industry, does their customer base mainly consist of one type or size of business (and if so does this concur with yours)?

Ensure that they are aware that you have prepared a brief

(assuming that you have). You will need copies of the website design brief with you; I would expect them to ask questions and discuss what you want, even if not in any great detail (as they are expecting to see the brief). You can provide answers from the brief (don't be afraid to look it up in the document, you are not being tested) and if you feel reasonably positive toward them you can provide a copy of the brief at the end of the meeting and ask them to provide a proposal. You may, on the other hand, decide to interview them all and then send copies of the brief when you decide on your final shortlist.

In addition to their capacity to provide what you are looking for, one of the main things you are trying to get out of the meetings is the need to 'click' somehow (sorry for the pun) with them. Like any service that requires the provider to gain an understanding of you and your business, you need to ensure that you get on well and can communicate clearly with them. If they talk in jargon leaving you clueless as to what has or hasn't been agreed, then even if they are the best designers in the world it is unlikely to be a good partnership. Do not forget that you are entrusting them with your business's future. You need to be able to communicate to ensure that you will have an outcome that meets *your* needs.

Review proposals

Set a date for receipt of proposals. Some may prefer to send them in writing, whether in print or by email; others may request the opportunity to present them to you. It is up to you what you choose, but in my opinion it is valuable to hear what they have to say. It is another opportunity to interact with them and ask questions.

Reach a decision and commission

How to decide? Before you make the commission, remember to check that their work schedule has not changed at this point. (They may have accepted a number of other contracts since you last met and their schedule might be full.)

By now you will be familiar with the criteria, and only you can make this decision. It should take into consideration that you are likely to have an extended working relationship with this company. It is not like getting your hair cut or commissioning a brochure which is very much a 'job and finish'. A website – by definition – is never finished. It will, of course, at a given point be deemed complete and published, but is then continuously in a state of change, always being reviewed or updated with current information.

In my experience, the more successful outcomes arise out of choosing a company with whom you are able to communicate and can envisage a good working relationship with and who are keen to help your business, rather than with a company who has seen and done it all before and treats you as just another contract.

10

SO HOW MUCH IS THIS GOING TO COST ME?

I am often asked the question, "What should I expect to pay for a website to be developed?" There is no definitive answer to this because, of course, it depends on what outcomes and functionality you require and what standards you expect to be met.

The alternative answer to this question is, that like any business investment, you need to consider what return you are likely to make on it. For every quote you get for a few thousand, you will find someone apparently willing to do the same thing (or so they say) for a few hundred. If this is the case, why not just go with the cheapest? After all, you might be a person who finds 'value' baked beans to be perfectly adequate and do not think there is any difference in designer label clothes.

Irrespective of advice, there will always be the 10 per cent overall who will buy the cheapest. As you may recall me commenting about other points, this is nothing to do with the internet. A well known marketing statistic is that, in any given market, approximately 10 per cent will buy the cheapest or want a bargain. At the other end of the scale, there are another 10 per cent who will pay a lot of money because they want the best and perceive that is the way to get it. Then there are the rest of us, the 80 per cent in the middle who want value for money, who will make a choice based on quality, convenience or some set of criteria.

One thing is for sure, if you go too cheap, you may not just be risking the money that you actually spend; you may be risking your business.

I was recently asked to work on a new project that involved offline as well as online promotion of a multi-million pound Business to Consumer (B2C) investment. The business was already trading when I was contacted, but had experienced some changes early on and now intended to build a new brand which could be rolled out across the UK and possibly beyond.

They had calculated that, in order to be in profit, they needed to turn over one million pounds per year. The variables for a proper marketing budget obviously vary wildly according to markets and will also vary through the life cycle of the product or business, but are likely to be higher at the beginning. However, it is generally accepted that a budget for a B2B needs to be between 2 and 10 per cent of sales (turnover), and that for a B2C market – especially retail and pharmaceuticals – the budget requirements can exceed 20 per cent, particularly during peak brand building years.

This means that as this was a new brand, in a B2C retail environment they would probably be looking at spending between £20,000 and £200,000 on marketing and promotion per year. After some consideration, I planned to recommend that for such a big project, they should be sourcing and contracting a very experienced design and advertising company, who had specific experience and a proven track record in their industry. That they would probably need to set a minimum budget of around £50,000 (this is very con-servative, just 5 per cent of projected turnover) for the creation of the brand identity and imagery. Since the website was not going to be a large part of their marketing – it was to be more of a corporate site in the first instance – then 10 per cent maximum of this budget (£5,000) was to be set aside for the website development.

This might appear to be a large spend, but when you consider that Heinz has recently spent £3.5 million on developing and marketing a new product variation[1] (and they are now in a legal dispute over the name, which is going to cost them even more) then it starts to put it into perspective.

However, while investigating the feasibility of the project, it came to my attention that someone in the company had already taken it upon themselves to contract the creation of a corporate identity for the brand. Unbelievably, he had followed the advice of a complete stranger he met in the local pub, who had recommended a 'bloke he knew, who is into design'.

This is a completely absurd situation, gambling on someone who may well be a good designer, but potentially has no track record or reputation in the industry, and entrusting him with the entire future of the company. As I write this, it is starting to sound made up – but really, this is true. This is not the first time I have encountered such situations. There is no question that if this business succeeds, it will be pure luck.

In the context of a small business, the figures are often vastly different, but the principle still applies. If your business has an annual turnover of £100,000, you should be considering that, according to what type of industry you are operating in, approximately 10 per cent (which is equal in this case to £10,000) should be your budget for marketing for the year. This will, of course, vary according to the industry and the current state of the market: if it is highly competitive, or constantly in acquisition by its nature, your budget needs to be higher as you have continually to maintain your positioning in order to compete. It will also depend on where your company or product currently stands in its development or life-cycle –

---

1. As reported in the Independent, 19/10/07 "Heinz soup range under attack from farmers' markets and MPs" by Martin Hickman. Source:
http://news.independent.co.uk/uk/politics/article3075674.ece.

it is often more expensive to establish than maintain a brand – so more money is needed at the beginning. Never under-estimate what is required to make a business successful. The marketing that a company invests today, this month, this year, means sales tomorrow, next week, or in the future.

So you might have contacted a number of different companies and found that their proposals very widely. Why are the charges so disparate? Consider the competitive nature of the industry. There were over 55,000 applicants on creative arts and design courses in UK universities in 2006[2], not counting computer science, e-commerce and media studies students. Of those who finish university each year in the UK, a proportion will not be able to find a job and will take the self-employed/freelance route instead, even if only in the short term. The web design world is very attractive from the outside. There are few barriers to entry, no regulation, computers are now cheap and you can work from home wherever that is.

This means that there are an awful lot of new inexperienced web designers out there every year. All competing for the same work, most of them competing only on price since so few have any other credibility such as an impressive customer base (gosh look who else they have worked for and they are really successful), shiny offices (they must be doing well and therefore are really good in order to afford this) to leverage the purchase.

So how much can you really expect to be getting for your investment?

Let's take the example of a new graduate who starts up as a web designer.

Assuming that he or she works from home, having annual fixed costs of only £1,000 (which for any business, let alone a technology business is very low) and that working time will be 5 days per week for 48 weeks of the year.

---

2. Source UCAS.

Now a new business would be doing very well to have work that amounts for 70 per cent of their actual capacity and anyone who has worked as a freelancer or run a sole trader business will be aware that you cannot be doing productive work all of the time. There is admin (taking at least half a day per week) and sales (taking at least one day per week) to be accommodated.

Developing and publishing websites brings a project cost also: domain names, hosting, server-side costs, etc. We can estimate these to be approximately 10 per cent of the value of a web design project.

For the web designer to project earnings of just £15,000 per annum (before tax) – which is a fairly meagre salary but not too bad for new graduates who perhaps don't yet want to start paying back their student loans – the daily rate charged must be in the region of £150 to cover the costs mentioned above.

So if you commission a website for £600, the maximum time that can be spent on it – including meetings, travelling time, research, talking to you on the phone, answering queries or pestering you for the content – is just four days.

What exactly can you expect an inexperienced, wet-behind-the-ears, straight-from-college designer to produce in four days? You might be lucky and have found someone who is brilliant; it is much more likely that you have not.

Bearing in mind the list of skills that we looked at in the previous chapter, where we considered if we would be equipped to carry out the job ourselves, do you think that in addition to having those skills such a designer is realistically going to be able to:

- Gain a full understanding of your objectives?

- Research your industry in order to gain an understanding of your target customers' behaviour?

- Interpret your existing brand identity – or worse try to develop a new one?

- Create an aesthetic design and layout that conveys your brand values and USP while appealing to your target market?

- Develop a logical information hierarchy and navigational structure for the site?

- Actually build the site and ensure that all the code functions correctly?

- Ensure that the site meets usability and accessibility criteria (as mentioned earlier, the latter of which is a legal requirement)?

- Optimize your site for search engines, ensuring that page titles, keywords and descriptions are all in place while advising you on the text content or indeed writing or rewriting the copy for you?

- Test the website in a real-world environment with a number of users that fit your target criteria?

This is the job that web designers should do. Remember that the task list above does not include any clever technology, anything on your wish list nor does it include illustrations, photography, programming scripts, plug-in technology, setting up third-party software such as a content management system (for you to update the content yourself in the future) or shopping cart and credit card transactions. Your web developer may or may not be able to provide some or all of these things mentioned above, but should certainly be able to obtain them or recommend to you where to go.

So what if you go to an established freelance web designer who has lots of experience and a proven track record? There is likely to be far more expenditure: the running of an office to take into account; maybe an assistant or at least part-time administrator; an accountant to do the bookkeeping and tax returns; a car and a reasonable expectation to earn the national average of around £25,000 per year before tax. Doesn't sound unreasonable to me.

This person is likely to spend a little more work time on sales, maybe two days per week and, if successful, might even be busy for 90 per cent of the designated work capacity. Of course, there might also be an expectation of more than the minimum 20 days per year holiday (including bank holidays).

For this designer to undertake a project worth £600 it would have to be completed in 1¼ days. Of course, the experienced designer knows that it is not possible to deliver a quality or even adequate result in such a short time so is very unlikely even to consider this project. Even a commission worth £2,000 has to be completed in just over five days. Since the admin and invoicing are carried out by someone else there is more time to concentrate on the work, but even for an experienced designer this is quite a short period of time.

Whichever way the designer charges, it is reasonable to expect the charging method to be transparent. The most common ways of charging are either by time (by the hour or day for each person involved in the development) or by the item: number of pages, functions or facilities, etc.

This is similar to many industries. For example, if you needed new windows in your house or office building, you could either contract a building company or carpenter who would be likely to charge you by the day for the number of people on site, or if you go to a double glazing company they usually charge by the item, i.e. they make some calculation based on the size of each window, the number of openings, and any special features such as coated glass, tilt and turn, window locks, etc.

The moral of the story: you get what you pay for.

11

COMMISSIONING AND CONTRACTING THE WEB DEVELOPMENT COMPANY

Friends of mine recently moved house and decided to have a completely new bathroom. So they got all the catalogues, looked on the internet and eventually drove down to a shop selling bathroom suites and fittings and ordered everything the salesman said they would need. They also found some lovely marble tiles that were expensive but beautiful and these were to be applied to the floor and walls.

Taking a referral from another friend they contacted a building and plumbing company who agreed to take on the contract. The company visited to survey the job and followed up with a quote. The quote seemed reasonable, so they were employed. They mentioned a contract to the builder who assured them that it was not necessary; they would have to pay extra for it and it would delay the work. Since they had been recommended this company, and they were waiting for the new bathroom to be fitted (by now there was a bath that had been delivered ahead of schedule sitting in the middle of their lounge), they went ahead thinking, "It'll be all right."

A whole series of problems ensued due to the fact that they did not have a specific and legal agreement with the builder.

The workmen didn't turn up on the day they promised and costs escalated: when they pulled up the old tiles, the builder said they would need a new sub-floor, then new pipe-work, then new electrics. They drilled the hole for the taps in the bath in the wrong place, no apology was offered, only a, "But they always go there," response when they complained. They clearly didn't know how to set up and fit the machinery of the new Jacuzzi bath – even though they had been told (verbally) that this is what was ordered – and broke something, so a new part had to be sourced causing a delay.

At this point an interim invoice arrived in the post, and even though they had not agreed to any kind of stage payments, they were pressured into paying it by being told that the builder wouldn't be able to pay his workers this week if they didn't.

This was the only bathroom in the house and, as time went on, and showering at the gym wore a bit thin, they became a little more impatient and demanding of the builder, who by now had started work on other jobs that had been scheduled in.

Finally they ran out of patience at the incompetence and unreasonable behaviour of the builder and, after having to purchase more marble for the second time as the workmen had broken many tiles due to using the wrong tool for cutting, they sacked the firm. They then received a further invoice for the whole job plus a long list of fittings and materials that they knew nothing about and had not been mentioned in the original quote.

This invoice remains outstanding and they have recently received a solicitor's letter and then one from a debt collection agency regarding this payment. They have had to contract another builder to complete the bathroom fitting, and have incurred far more costs than were necessary, not to say inconvenience and stress.

If they had not made any assumptions, had put everything in writing and had a contract that included clauses to deal with unforeseen problems, extra work, circumstances under which payment could be withheld and so on, they would not now be in this situation. They were promised the job to be finished in two weeks – almost two years later it is still dragging on. Before them lies the possibility of going to court and the unknown costs that may be incurred with legal representation not to mention the stress.

It seems that more assumptions are made when contracting design work than even when contracting builders. This is where you have to reach a specific and detailed agreement to ensure that you are completely clear about what is going to be carried out: who is going to do what, how and when it will happen, what will be paid and what provision is there for after the work is complete. In addition, what will happen if things do not go exactly as planned? The number of times I have heard, "Well we just said that we liked the design ideas and the website is going ahead," followed by, "What do you mean contract?"

As with all business transactions – in particular the supply of services – it is important that there is some sort of legal contract in place with your supplier or customer to ensure that any future problems are provided for before the transaction is complete. I cannot stress strongly enough that you should always consult with qualified legal advisors to ensure that all aspects are covered. Engaging a solicitor to oversee a contract supplied by the web design company or to draw up a contract if they do not supply one may seem expensive in the overall scheme of things, but could turn out to be relatively inexpensive considering the fees that would be charged should a legal dispute arise.

Legal stuff
Note that this is not a definitive specification as each project will be different, and, as stated above, you should consult qualified legal advice.

As a guide, in the contract that should be supplied by the developer you would expect to see information of some details of:

- What exactly is going to be carried out. Will the company:

  o Research your competitors and provide a report, identify keywords and so on?

  o Produce illustrations, take photographs, write the copy?

  o Or are they only going to carry out the minimum requirements of actually designing, coding and uploading the site?

  o Do you have to arrange for your own domain name and hosting services or are they going to do this? (Many designers like to work with one host. This is not usually about making a commission on the sale but because they are familiar with their ways of working. It is exactly the same in the design-for-print world where designers normally have relationships with a specific printer, as they know how they work, and understand their technology and scheduling parameters, which all makes the job less problematic and ensures consistent outcomes.)

  o Who is going to update the website? If you are and a database or content management system is specified, will you require training on the use of this, will this be included and how long will it take?

- What the website is for, how it is expected to function, what criteria it must meet (if any).

- What constraints affect the project, an estimate of the expected number of pages, timescales, etc.

- Prices and payment terms including details of any stage payments.

- Extra work – what happens if there are any changes to the

agreed scope of the project or if any changes are requested along the way?

- Liabilities – who is liable if something goes wrong or if the company reputation is damaged in some way or experiences a loss of business etc.?

- Withholding of payment for remedial work and under what terms and for what period this is likely to be.

- Intellectual property – who will own the rights to the website, and to the designs and content contained therein?

- The future – additional work, updates and changes; future charges may be subject to change; the length of this contract. etc

- Any other terms and conditions necessary to deal with your specific project or requirements.

Intellectual property and the copyright to your website
Intellectual property has intrinsic value and like all property can be sold or leased for a business return. It comes into being through some kind of creative or intellectual activity including design. Copyright is concerned with the protection of the expression of an idea, rather than the process by which it came about.[1]

Any kind of IP is a minefield when it comes to the internet. The differing viewpoints of the designers and the client must be resolved in each individual case. It is perfectly normal for clients to assume that they 'own' the website that they have commissioned and paid for. However, the law does not see it this way. Intellectual property law and, more specifically, copyright law is automatically assigned, and the rights to the

---

1. For more information on intellectual property in the UK see the Patent Office website at http://www.ipo.gov.uk/whatis.htm.

designs and ideas that are expressed in a website are automatically owned by its originator – the web designer. The
same law applies to graphic, textile or fashion designers, as it
does to an author who has written a book or poem, or to a
composer or songwriter. Unlike trademarks or patents, this is
not something that has to be applied for. It is automatic, and
many originators of work will simply note their claim to the
copyright by using the © mark on a document or similar.

It is worth noting perhaps that copyright law is not new and
certainly not a recent invention of designers. It originated in
1732 when William Hogarth (1697 – 1763) was outraged at
the piracy of his engravings from his own series of paintings
entitled 'A Harlot's Progress'. He initiated the first Act of
Parliament that protected the copyright of engravers and
designers. This act was known as Hogarth's Act and later as
Hogarth's law.

The rights of web designers to their intellectual property
have followed on from how traditional and then digital
graphic design was handled. Put concisely, the designers
would always own the work, and the right to be known as the
creator of the work (called their moral rights) but they would
also grant the rights to use the work, in a specific medium or
media, in a given geographical area and for a given period of
time. This might mean that the designers created a design for
a brochure and licensed it for such use, but did not license the
imagery to be used in a poster, on TV or on the internet. This
is something that is important to note when using any existing
imagery that has been created for you by other designers. If
the web design company is expected to use it or interpret it for
the web, you need to provide permission – in writing – from
the originator of the work to the web design company.

If you want to own the rights to the website and/or specific
photographs, illustrations, imagery, etc., then this must be
specifically stated in the contract. Remember that you cannot
make unreasonable demands and it is the designers' preroga-
tive to be in control of this. There are many business advisors

out there who state categorically that you should demand the copyright to the website. These are often the words of someone who does not have a sufficiently clear understanding of copyright and the design industry. But it is a little more complicated than this in practice. For you to own *all* rights to the website, then there may be other rights that exist down the chain of creativity and production. For example, if you have produced the copy, you own the rights automatically. If you have commissioned the copy from a copywriter, then you may well have the rights assigned to you.

However, if you have all rights rigidly assigned, then this means that, in theory, the copywriter could not ever reuse a generic sentence, like one that invites enquiries and says that a representative will endeavour to respond within 24 hours or one working day, etc. Now clearly this would be unreasonable. It does not specifically apply to your company and there are only so many ways of saying "thank you for contacting us".

What about photographs? If you have specifically commissioned photographs to be taken on your behalf, it is reasonable for you to own the rights to them and, if they are specific to your company (maybe photos of your staff, or your offices), it is reasonable to expect that they would not be used for any other purpose. However, it is common in the design and photography industries to use stock photography; these are photographs taken by a professional and then offered for sale for use in a variety of formats for a variety of uses. This is a relatively cheap way of obtaining a photo, particularly of a generic subject, or one where a specific subject matter might not be practical. For example, photos of models, sunsets or landscapes. Have a trawl around the internet. Many websites are decorated with photographs that are at best relevant and underpin the message, or at worst gratuitous. The majority of photos you see are not individually commissioned or the rights are not owned by the company whose website it is, rather it is more likely that the designers have obtained limited rights to use that particular photo online for a fraction of the cost of the full rights to the photo.

The same applies to web designers. If the company commissioning the site design is insisting on the full rights to all the designs and other items subject to copyright contained within, it is going to be very much more expensive than otherwise.

The process – what to expect

All designers are likely to follow a slightly different process when it comes to the detail, but it is probably something like the following order of production. Note that there are stages which should be approved by you, the client, before the next stage is begun. This should be detailed in the designers' terms and conditions and they often correspond to the stage payments.

The first stage would involve *discussion* with the designers asking questions about your business, and you supplying *information* and copies of anything that is already in use, details of your competitors and things that you like, preferably in the form of a design brief (see Chapter 8, Communicating with Your Web Designers or Developers).

The designers may then produces '*roughs*'. These might be manual or digital sketches that are shown to you to discuss whether they are on the right track.

Any experienced web design or development team would work to *project plans* and be scheduling work in order to maximize their output. A project plan of what will happen and to what timescale should be provided. This may not necessarily be that detailed. It might be a weekly action plan, for example:

- Week 1: Domain name to be registered and hosting set up.

- Week 2: Client to provide copies of all existing marketing material and everything relating to current corporate image including any permissions needed; supplementary information regarding customers and competitors.

- Week 4: Draft designs for sample web page to be presented and approved.

You get the idea.

Once these are approved, a *draft* of an actual webpage or pages will be submitted. This may be the home page or the home page and another page if there is to be a significant difference in the structure. It will be very close in appearance to the finished website but will probably not function (the buttons or links will not go anywhere and so on). This is your chance to make comments or voice concerns. It is also the time to consider some possible 'walk-through' testing with real people who are not involved with the project.

Before your designers carry out this stage and provide the design for the site, you should supply some *draft* text for the home page or another page. It does not need to be the final copy, but should be representative. Ensure that you make it clear that it is draft text, and that you want them to use it when they lay the design out. They may object or say there is no need but you should insist.

Most designers use what is often called 'the Greek text' or 'lorem ipsum' (as those are the first two words of the pseudo-Latin passage). Commonly employed to create page layouts it is a passage of text that doesn't mean anything. It is placed where the text will eventually go and formatted according to the design. This is normal practice in graphic as well as web design. However, there is a disadvantage in assessing the design with the Greek text still in place; there is a tendency to ignore whether the text is legible as you make no attempt to read beyond the first two words because you can't (it's not even real Latin). Having some real text in place – even though you change it later – will give you a much better impression of how your website will appear to your customers and whether the text is actually legible.

Either after this stage or at the same time, a *hierarchical plan* of the structure and navigation for the site will be produced. This is likely to be shown on the form of a diagram and the navigation will be seen on the draft webpage sample(s). Note that many designers will take your approval of this hierarchy as set in stone; it can often represent a lot of extra work to alter or add to a hierarchy (depending on the way the website is built).

The next stage would be the *construction* of the entire site. This would be a completed but empty (of content) site. In other words, all the pages would be made, the navigation would be functioning, the pages will look like the finished product, but there will no content, or it will contain sample content. Some designers include guidance notes on the pages at this stage which will be replaced by the real content.

The *content* must now be supplied so you should have been working hard on this before the site construction is completed. The designers will now be waiting for you. The content (text, images, etc.) needs to be supplied in the form specified by the designers or you may incur extra cost if there is any manipulation, file conversion or similar work required (usually easy but very time consuming). Of course, if your site is to be database-driven you may be going to input the content yourself, so it would be at this point or before where you would supply a sample of content for testing purposes.

Once the content is supplied and included in the site, the website should then be *checked* for any minor detail or changes required. At this stage we should only be talking about small stuff: typographical errors (typos), spelling, punctuation, some detail on the wrong page, this type of thing. Be careful to be sure here, as anything you ask for after this stage is likely to incur a charge and be considered extra work to the original contract (unless, of course, it is some error on the part of the designers).

Once any *final changes* are made, the signing off or approval of the finished product takes place. This is what is going to be online for the world to view.

Assuming that the content is completed (and you are not going to be inputting details of your 50,000 stock items for the next three months) the site is then *published* (more details on this in Chapter 14, Publish and Promote).

Any required or agreed *training* on the updating of the database or content management system would take place (if it hadn't already) and you would be publishing the site yourself (as per the instructions you would have been given).

The website project would now be considered to be *completed* and the final payment would now be due.

There is, of course, an ongoing part of the overall process, where I contradict the previous sentence by saying that a website is never finished. This is the updating process. If it is to be carried out via your database then you (or someone working for you) will be carrying this out on a regular basis. If the site is not of that type but requires a regular update, then you might be trained to use a content management system. These are very easy to use; most people learn everything they need to know in a few hours. Of course, experience will increase competency on this.

Otherwise the website will be updated as per your agreement, i.e. on request or at regular intervals. This may be included in the price for the first year, or may be charged separately according to how much needs to be updated.

By covering all aspects of the plan before embarking on the project you will be much more likely to have a successful outcome and, if a problem or dispute arises, you will have agreed in advance how to deal with it. And hopefully you will enjoy a long, happy and profitable relationship with your web development company.

12

THE LANGUAGE OF THE CUSTOMER

You never get a second chance to make a first impression. When you walk into that initial business meeting or interview with a long sought-after customer for the first time you are probably nervous. You have pressed your suit and polished your shoes or carefully considered whether this outfit is suitable or if that jewellery is too much. However you want to appear, the conveying of your ability or capacity to deliver is tied up in those first few critical minutes. It has often been said that people buy from people, not businesses, and in a business to business (B2B) environment this can be a critical time. You might have read up on body language or even been on some kind of sales training or business networking course to improve your interpersonal skills.

If you are operating in a business to consumer (B2C) market, you probably are aware that billions are spent every year on revamping shop frontages, on the specific layout and merchandising of the products for sale, or on creating just the right atmosphere within the shop from music to lighting.

The old adage that you never get a second chance to make a first impression is particularly true when applied to websites. Taking into account user behaviour on the internet, the amount of effort that you put in to making the right first impression is even more critical. Recent research indicates that, on average, users spend no more than 27 seconds on a single webpage, and often only around 10 seconds on the home page or whatever is the first page they encounter on any particular website.

People come to websites to find out information: information on how to do something; information on a product, information on your company. In fact, in a B2B situation, the internet has become the number one place to find out further information before considering doing business with a particular company. You might be thinking that people also go to websites to play games, make contact with friends and so on. This is very true, but in the context of this book, we are talking about business and meeting your business objectives through your website.

Since people go to websites to find out information, it would be misguided not to provide information in an easy to read and use form. This chapter addresses what content to include and how to ensure that the text content (copy) for your website is effective.

In an ideal world, I would recommend without hesitation that you employ the services of an experienced website copywriter who has a proven track record in your industry or with your target customer. However, this is not always possible and, even if your budget allows for this, in order to project manage the website development effectively, you still need to have an overview of the context within which you are working.

Let's start with the home page. As well as providing the world with a window through which to look at your business, it has many roles. It can be the magazine or brochure cover, tempting the reader to enter and read more. It could be thought of as the front door, entrance, hallway or lobby or even receptionist to your online environment, helping users to create a mental map of where they can go and what they can do. The home page should be considered the hardest working page of all, but also where the most compromises are made.

So should you welcome your visitors? Although fashionable in the late 1990s it is no longer necessary or appropriate – and now one of the things that people dislike about websites (see Chapter 1, What is Wrong with the current Website?). Therefore don't say 'welcome' or 'welcome to our website' or 'welcome to the website of company x' or invite people to 'look around our website to…'. You get the picture. Nor is there ever a need to use the word 'website' when referring to your website – people know that they are online. It is also a problem if you find that you need to give people instructions on how to use your website – in fact, if you need to give instructions on how to use your site then you need to redesign it!

Your first goal is to ensure that your visitors immediately know where they are or that they have arrived in the right place. This can usually be effectively achieved through the prominent display of your company logo, name and tagline or strapline (the brief statement that tells people what you do, or in many cases is designed to express the core values of your business). The best place for this is always near the top and convention states that it would normally be on the top left.[1]

A word about sticking to conventions, which I've mentioned before. People use other websites more than they use yours (since there are billions of them out there) so while you might like to think of yourself as innovative and therefore want your website to be innovative, think again. Your website will be more successful if it is easy to use. Anything unconventional, novel or innovative requires users to learn how to use it. This hampers them and is more likely to make them go away and look for an easier place to find out this information than be impressed. Who in their right mind would have a maze, puzzle entrance or similar in the entrance to their shop? They are more likely to have wide easy-to-traverse doors that open automatically as you approach, tempting smells or products attractively displayed near the entrance. Hopefully

---

1. More than 70 per cent of websites have their logo in the top left corner.

you took this on board in Chapter 1, if not I hope you are getting the idea!

You need to communicate the purpose of the site clearly. Usually in the case of a business website this would mean simply stating what you do, in as few words as possible, near to the top of the page or main page content. This may seem obvious while reading this book, however, many websites are so littered with marketing speak and waffle that they fail to convey any real information. For example, can you guess what the following business does?

The company tagline:
High performance. Delivered.

The main text on their home page – word for word:
Organizations achieve unconventional results through unconventional approaches.

The only text other than links:
High performance starts here.
Improving business performance through a revitalized workforce.
Company x and company y sign multiyear business services agreement.

And not much better on the services page:
Committed to delivering innovation, [company x] collaborates with its clients to help them achieve high performance. Our professionals leverage leading-edge technologies and tools to identify new opportunities . . . blah blah blah

Any idea what any of that means? Me neither. It is all marketing blather and waffle with no substance. What a wasted opportunity. I wonder exactly who searches on 'leverage leading-edge technologies' or 'unconventional approaches'. It is not so difficult to say simply what you do, or what users (customers) can do (if anything) on the website. Remember you probably have less than 10 seconds to convince them to stay on your site or they will just click the back button and off they go to one of the other billion or so websites online.

So how do we do this? By applying a few straightforward principles and a little knowledge on how people read online, we can create concise usable text for your website.

People just do not read all the text. They instead have information-seeking behaviour and will scan a page looking for something that might possibly lead them to what they are looking for. Your website will be no exception. Eye-tracking studies show that instead of reading whole sentences, people read the first few words of a sentence or paragraph and then skip over the rest of the text to the next one.

This gives us a clear action point: ensure that the first few words in a sentence or start of a paragraph clearly convey what the paragraph is about.

As mentioned above, avoid marketing speak, waffle, fluff (add any other word for it you like here) or any words whose purpose is just to pad the page out; in fact, don't use any words that have no specific purpose or do not convey specific information.

Avoid jargon. Speak in language that your customers or potential customers can understand. Use a conversational tone unless it is really not appropriate. If jargon or technical language is unavoidable, always provide links to a glossary of terms or use some other facility to explain the terms. You might argue that your website provides technical information to a technical industry, and the users of your website will always be highly educated in their subject. This may be so, but the people who are in that technical industry were all novices at some point and setting barriers to entry will help no-one, least of all your business.

On this point, you need use as simple and plain a style and

language as is practical in your given situation. The purpose of your website is not to demonstrate how clever you are, but to promote your business in some way. With this in mind, remember that no-one likes being talked down to or patronized. Paying attention to your target audience can help with this. Have you ever bought two different newspapers on the same day and read a report of the same incident? You might have noticed that the reporting was so different it could have been a completely different event. This is because the newspapers are highly focused and have detailed research on the type of readership they are targeting and have tailored their style to maintain this customer base.

During the process of researching your customer (as discussed in Chapter 4, Who is the Website for Anyway?) you should have identified the general nature of your customer profile including their level of language use. For example, is it a domestic mass market or are you offering products or services to adults who are more likely to be high earners and therefore educated? Is your target and industry sector likely to include engineers or technical users? It is an obvious thing to say, but easy to forget, that you need to tailor the content to the people you expect to use the site in terms of readability as well as actual content.

The readability of a website can make a big difference in whether you effectively communicate your message. The term readability describes how easy or difficult it is to understand a sentence, passage or page of text. Anything that improves the readability will enable a wider range of users to understand your website content. That said, if you are focusing on a narrow customer profile or targeting a very specific type of user, then the readability needs to be tailored to them. There are a variety of different ways of measuring readability; most use some kind of formula or algorithm that is a function of the number of words per sentence and the number of syllables per word. The broader the market at which you are aiming, the lower the readability needs to be. So the rule of thumb is, for readers whose level you are unable to predict or to ensure that your website can be understood by the broadest range of users, use shorter sentences and simpler words.[2]

The information should be structured so that the reader will quickly understand what the item is about. As I said earlier, website users often only read the first half of the first sentence of a paragraph and so it is crucial that there are keywords contained in this area that quickly convey the content of this paragraph, giving readers a reason to continue or return. This also works for search engine robots. The higher up the keyword, the more importance it is given. Structuring the information so that the important details are at the top, with less crucial or subsidiary information lower down, is sometimes described as 'inverse pyramid'. This is commonly used in news reporting but is in opposition to traditional writing construction where an introduction, a presentation of all the facts and finally a conclusion are the norm.

The actual information you include in the website also needs to be set out from the customer's viewpoint, not that of your business. You may have departments in your business that deal with different parts of your production process, but it is not acceptable to structure your website information like this. It needs to be organized in a way that your customer experiences it.

For example, imagine that your company deals with the worldwide distribution of DVDs to both the trade and the domestic market. Now as there are different technical formats, commercial issues such as release dates as well as legal issues relating to different parts of the world, then your business may well be structured according to region, e.g. UK, US, Asia, Europe, etc. Individuals who simply want to purchase the latest Hollywood blockbuster movie might not be aware of regional differences so this would not be an appropriate structure to

---

2. There is a free website readability checker at http://www.readability.info/ that will measure a single webpage against a number of readability standards – of course you may need to do a bit of study to interpret the results.

make visible to them. Of course, you will need to collect information on which region they are located in, but the first impression they see on your website should not be to do with geographic location and DVD formats. It should be to do with latest releases and offers available in their region (which has been identified in the background) that tempt them to buy.

What if you sell to both a domestic and trade or technical market? Maybe you have a website that sells cameras both to the general public and to the professional photographic industry. In this case careful consideration is required. You could develop a site that has a clear area for professionals and another for the public with a different type of style and level of detail in each. However, as many businesses have found to their loss, this can confuse the user at the very first stage. How many users find themselves hesitating when faced with the choice found on so many websites that sell IT or office equipment. Two options are offered: 'home office' or 'small business'. What if you are a small business that works from home? This is more common every day (both people working from home and confusing choices). Try to think of all the types of people who might be your customers and how they would fit into your categories – more importantly how they might categorize themselves.

One way to deal with this is to present the information in a layered way. This means providing summaries or reduced level of detail at the initial presentation, with links offered to more detailed levels of technical information. This both avoids the basic user being overwhelmed with jargon and provides those who need more information, in order to be able to make an informed choice, with access to the detail they crave.

On this subject, one thing to avoid is the practice of chopping up related or continuous information to make short chunks – page 1, page 2, page 3, etc., and then providing a 'next' or 'next page' link at the bottom. This makes the information cumbersome to read, difficult to copy and everyone we surveyed hated it, finding it generally irritating and 'out of kilter' with using the web.

Another point to note is the use of files provided in pdf format (acrobat files). This has been mentioned before as one of the things that people hate most about websites. In case you are not familiar with this, acrobat or pdf is a type of file created by the company Adobe that is used to distribute documents electronically. The beauty of it is that the reader program needed is distributed free and is often pre-installed on new computers. The problem with it is that it does not behave like a website, is not usually designed for reading on the screen, is often used to distribute brochures that contain lots of full colour pages and eats up lots of the users' ink (without warning them first) when printed. It also launches a program in order to view the acrobat (pdf) file. If this happens without warning – as it so often does – it can crash the user's computer. If you have any doubt as to how difficult acrobat files are to use, have a look at the one kindly provided (at the time of writing) by the patent office at http://www.ipo.gov.uk/myip.pdf. There are far worse pdfs around, but this is an example of a document that is clearly intended to be read in print. However, if you were to try to print it no ordinary office or desktop printer would be able to reproduce it effectively. It is not in A4 or letter paper proportions (which have ratio of approximately 8:11, this document's proportions are approximately 4:11 so requires tall narrow paper to print as it was intended), a quarter of the pages have a solid colour background and more than half have a quarter of the page or more as a photo or other solid colour illustration. This would use up a lot of ink for no purpose, in particular when you consider how little actual information is in it. Even though the information contained in the document is very valuable, it is just not accessible. Evidently no-one has considered who will be using this document and the circumstances in which they require the information.

Use clear and appropriate terms for headings and titles. Meaningless headings such as 'what to do next?' are a lost opportunity to include a keyword which will attract the attention of both the user and the search engines. This is particularly important for navigation – buttons or links to other pages or sources of information. Don't use any made-up words or invented phrases. If you must use abbreviations or acronyms – possibly because they are too long – ensure that they are explained *on the same page* by the use of alt text or similar. While users hate things that pop up, no explanation of an acronym is worse.

I recently heard that there had been changes to how a specific business allowance is to be handled so I went to the web address provided by the news service to have a look at the detail. In the first sentence there was a three-letter acronym that meant nothing to me and I could not find an explanation anywhere in the website. Apart from wasting my time, this is a completely unacceptable situation in a website that is supposed to be providing a public service. I for one am very unlikely to return to that particular site looking for information as my initial experience of it resulted in confusion and frustration. Imagine the effect of a similar experience on a website that is intended to sell products directly to the buyers. In general, those users who have had a bad experience the first time never return unless the persuasion is very powerful.

Captions and other text detail are required for all images (except those that are purely decorative, which should in any case be kept to a minimum). Not only is this required in order to comply with accessibility rules and the Disability Discrimination Act (all images should have an accompanying alt text), it is a proven design principle that pictures and text together are more powerful in drawing attention and generating memory. As well as this, search engines favour images that have a text caption directly below them. Ensure that the caption or description makes sense. Imagine that you are describing it – as concisely as you can – to someone who cannot see the image.

There is a strong debate about repeated information on a

website. One side says that if you have said it once, then you should never repeat yourself. I would agree that this is true on any given page. However, you do need to consider that a high proportion of users entering your website are unlikely to enter at the home page. In fact it is reported that over 60 per cent of 'landing pages' (the page to which a search engine or other link sends a user) are pages *other* than the home page. This means that you cannot at any time have an expectation that someone will experience your website like a book, beginning at the start (the home page) and progressing through. The path that users take through a site, including the entry or landing page, and the exit page vary greatly. You need to ensure that whatever page users find themselves on, it makes sense in isolation and provides subsidiary information so that they will quickly get a sense of where they are. It should also provide suitable links to related information and enable users to have a sense of where they are in terms of the overall structure of the website. If ensuring this means repeating yourself, then definitely do so.

Whatever content, style or level of detail you are using you need to be consistent. Consistent in your use of language, consistent in the way the information is structured and consistent in how it is visually presented. Users learn very quickly (and without realizing) that a heading looks a particular way (bigger and bold or whatever) or that, if a word is underlined, it represents a link to another page. (As a general rule, all users think that underlined text represents a link to another page, so you should meet this expectation by using underlined text to do just this.) Sudden changes to different styles and conventions within the site – even if you think it is logical – can be jarring for users or raise doubt as to whether they have accidentally strayed to another website. If by the nature of your site you are sending them to a different website – maybe to make a payment or similar – then tell them. This way at least it is expected.

Although it is very much the designers' job to decide on the text formatting there are a few points that it is useful to be aware of. The text needs to be laid out logically and headings should be used to break up blocks of text. You can highlight keywords in the text using bold or similar – but not too often, if too many things are highlighted in some way nothing stands out. Beware of making all the text bold. It gives readers an impression of the text being very heavy-going and can put them off even beginning. Use bulleted lists when there are a number of points in no particular order, and numbered lists when there is a process or a logical order to be indicated. Exclamation marks have no place in professional writing, and writing text in all capital letters LOOKS LIKE YOU ARE SHOUTING.

Anyone who has ever been in sales or has been on some kind of sales training knows that a 'call to action' is necessary, in other words asking for the order, or prompting the website user to carry out some kind of action that results in a purchase or enquiry. Anyone who regularly uses the internet will agree that they are constantly bombarded with demands to 'buy NOW!' or 'CLICK HERE!!!!' and so on that they become at best immune or at worst averse to this type of visual prompting.

In general, consider your users, avoid the hard sell, use persuasion based on customer benefits and be open and transparent with detail and terms. Do everything you can to enable customers to make their own decisions based on the excellent content that you provide.

13

TESTING TESTING TESTING

In most industries that actually make something, the product is thoroughly tested before it is released for sale. For example, imagine a car that had not been subjected to the most rigorous safety testing before being allowed on the road or a child's toy on sale in Europe without the CE mark[1].

Admittedly, these examples may be primarily to do with safety or other regulations and are consequently attributed a high budget; understandable when whoever will be ultimately responsible – usually the business owner – considers the prospect of getting sued for damages if he has failed to give this sufficient attention.

There are plenty of examples of rigorous testing, from consumer products (did the focus group prefer the cheesy or salty crackers?) to finite elements analysis (a computer simulation technique used in engineering). However, the testing of a website rarely extends beyond the most cursory 'clicking around the site to see what happens' or maybe going as far as seeing what it looks like in another type of browser – which is commonly carried out by someone

---

1. CE marking is used by manufacturers to indicate something complies with the appropriate European Directives. For more information on CE marking see the Department for Business, Enterprise and Regulatory Reform (formerly the DTI) at http://www.berr.gov.uk/dius/innovation/regulations/cemark/page11646.html.

in, or who happens to be passing, the web designers' office.

This means that you are putting something out there, untested, for people to use, which can be accessed for free, all over the world and which represents the front line of your livelihood: your business. Is that such a good idea?

The best way?
The best way to get your website tested is undoubtedly by a professional. It has to be acknowledged, however, that this may not be advice that you have the budget to accommodate; or possibly doesn't fit in with the reasons that made you buy this book.

A DIY approach?
So let's have a look at the principles and processes involved in website testing; see what might be practical to contribute or carry out yourself; plan to facilitate the testing of your own website in order to get the best possible result given limited resources.

There are three main questions that need to be answered. Therefore there are three different kinds of testing that we need to carry out in order to ensure that we have made the best possible effort. The testing process is meant to help us to find answers to those questions. We cannot always do this definitively, but it can help us to build a picture of how the site is going to serve the business.

1. **Does it actually function?**
   The website needs to perform all of its intended functions in all foreseeable situations and circumstances. This type of testing is carried out near or at the end of the development process, although testing of individual items such as feedback forms would also be carried out as they were

developed and integrated into the website. This testing would include:

a) Hyperlinks that are between pages and also those that link out of the site – do they work and do they take you where they are supposed to?

b) Do all the images, pictures and diagrams appear on the page? It is not uncommon to find some files missing; this can be due to communication interruptions on uploading the site to the server. This can also be to do with the way the images are defined in the HTML for the page. It would probably not occur to most users that the images are not really 'in' the page. The HTML gives the browser instructions to 'go and get the image file from a particular location' and 'display it in a specific place on the page' complete with a defined set of attributes such as size, position, alt text, text wrapping etc.

c) Any active elements such as enquiry forms and, in particular, confirmation pages as these are often missed; when used they appear automatically after the user has clicked on the 'send form' (or similar) button to confirm to the user that something has indeed been sent. They often extract items that the user has completed in the form which are then inserted by the software into some standard text.

For example, you might see a page that says, *Thank you Mr Smith for sending us your enquiry. Someone will contact you to discuss your needs within 24 hours. When we contact you, we will use the following infor-mation: Mr Smith, ABC enterprises, johnsmith@abc.co.uk, 0123 456789* (or similar).

This can give the impression that there is someone at the receiving end replying to enquiries immediately. This can be a good thing and a bad thing: if you say you will reply within 24 hours, you need to do so; it also raises the question in the minds of the users that if there is someone there to answer an email, they might just as well talk to you now.

2. **Do your customers get it?**
    Does it communicate what it is supposed to? Is it easy to use? Can real people find their way around it, or it is too confusing for anyone to be able to complete the tasks or processes that your customers need to carry out?

    a) Can they identify in less than a minute what the site is for and what you are offering or what they can do on the site?

    b) Can they navigate around it easily without getting lost or repeating actions needlessly?

    c) Can they find the information that the site is intended to provide: how to contact you, what you sell or do, technical information on products, prices, terms, delivery, etc.?

    d) Can they carry out any appropriate functions: complete enquiry forms, make a purchase . . .?

    e) Do they find the experience of using the site to be easy or frustrating, clear or confusing?

3. **Can the search engines find it?**
    Does all the SEO effort result in the search engines finding it? There are three questions that we need to answer:

a) Do the search engines list your website?

b) What information do the search engines have about your website?

c) Where do you appear in the listings or results for your chosen (and well-researched) keywords?

We approach this in three ways:

- Optimization testing where we look at Google Info, available online – for free.
- Benchmarking test, including site statistics, search engine listings, referral listing, ranking checks.
- Ongoing testing – where we repeat the benchmark tests every month.

TESTING
Now we know what we are trying to find out, how is it done and, more importantly in the context of this book, how do we go about contributing to it?

What should your web designers be doing to test the site?
You would reasonably expect your web designers or developers to carry out testing. They should not put a site online that does not function. They should check that everything does what it should. After all, it is their responsibility to produce something that works and is fit for purpose. That said, sometimes it is not actually possible to check something until it is online, so there is a bit of a chicken and egg situation.

There is no harm in a little supplementary guerrilla testing of your own. It is free, will take a little of your time, and hopefully the time of a friend, colleague or technically savvy member of your family, who you just might be able to persuade to help you.

Inform the designers

If you intend to do this, inform the designers at the outset. It will cause fewer problems if they know what will be required at each stage (and they won't be able to throw any extra charges onto you). There can be a bonus effect of this strategy. If they think you are intending to carry out independent testing, it is possible that they may well be a little more careful about how they do things. Of course, we would assume that your designers would be professional at all times and carry out everything conscientiously and to the best of their abilities. Sadly experience shows this is not always the case.

DIY GUERRILLA TESTING
Seeking help with testing

When you seek out and choose an assistant to help you with the testing you need to find someone who is the right type and who is in the right kind of position. He or she needs to be the pernickety kind; the one in your office or family who points out the continuity mistakes in the TV programme, the one who crosses the 't's and dots the 'i's. The tester need not be a computer expert. In fact (as with user testing detailed later) this can be a disadvantage as instead of plainly looking at the site and working on it like a 'normal person' he or she would be likely to become a critic on the technical aspects, designs or methodologies applied in the site construction. This is not the time for this; we just need to know if what we have does its job.

Hardware and software for testing

You will need a computer (and one for your assistant assuming that you have found someone who is willing to help); suitable internet connections and software are obviously required.

Most people are working with Windows Internet Explorer as their web browser (the program that you use to look at websites). It will tell you in the title bar (the coloured bit at the top of the screen) what it is: first it gives the page title (as discussed in Chapter 6, Selecting Keywords to Target Your Customers) and then the name of the browser.

You can get more definitive details on the browser and the version by clicking on the help menu. Then usually at or near the bottom of the list it will say 'about ...', click on this and you will get details.

Testing in alternative browsers

As not everyone in the world is using the latest Microsoft Version (even though Microsoft would like to think they are) it would be beneficial to find another computer with an older version such as version 5 or 6. If you have an older computer at home or maybe in your offspring's bedroom it might have an older browser installed. Also you could download an alternative web browser onto a computer.

It is very easy to download another browser such as Opera (from http://www.opera.com/) or Firefox (from http://www. mozilla.com/en-US/firefox/) completely free of charge. Just go to the website and follow the instructions. That said, if we are talking about teenagers or pre-teens who like computers you can bet they have the latest version of everything that can be downloaded for free. So maybe you just need to ask them (or maybe offer some kind of bribe).

Just do it

Refer to the list above for the things you are looking for, and then just use the site thoroughly. You are looking for something that does not do what it should. So you need to ensure before you begin that you are clear on what should happen.

You need to click on every button, link, picture that enlarges or whatever other element is on the page. Use the back button constantly so that when you click on a button or link – say on the home page that takes you to the contact page – you check that you have gone to the correct page and then click on back to go back to the home page.

Tedious but easy. The hardest thing about doing this is staying awake and alert, and keeping track of what you have already done, so that you don't miss out anything.

Of course, if your web designers have taken heed of the most basic usability rule – to use links that change colour to show pages that have already been visited – then it won't be quite as hard. However, you still need to click on every link on every page, so you may need to take a few notes to keep track.

An easy thing to miss is a picture that should enlarge or give more information.

Check again anything that doesn't seem to work as it should and, if it still doesn't work, make a note of the problem and, in particular, the page it was on (without this the designers have no chance) and make a snagging list of bits and pieces for them.

Other tests – online for free

There are lots of other tests to do with the functioning of the site, but it would be more realistic for your web developers to carry these out, mainly because interpreting the results can be difficult. Still, there is no harm in being familiar with these, although web designers everywhere will now be tearing their hair out and I am likely to get death threats in the mail.

For example, you could verify the HTML (if you feel like it). This test is supposed to validate that the programming and all the code that goes on in the background is correct. This is normally taken to be a kind of quality assurance test, and usually checks

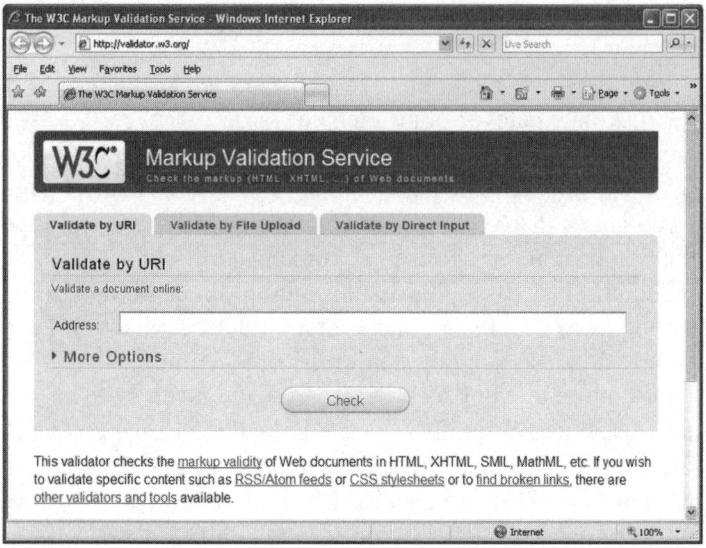

Fig. 12 How to verify the HTML code.

against the standards set by the World Wide Web Consortium[2].

There are lots of free checking systems out there, the definitive one being available from the World Wide Web Consortium at http://validator.w3.org/. It is easy to use. Just copy and paste the web address into the input box and click on the 'check' button. See Fig. 12.

That said, you are very unlikely to understand the results, and the big scary text it returns such as:

'This page is not Valid XHTML 1.0 Transitional!'

followed by:

'Failed validation, 71 Errors'

---

2. The World Wide Web Consortium (W3C) is an international consortium where Member organizations, a full-time staff, and the public work together to develop web standards. W3C's mission is: 'To lead the World Wide Web to its full potential by developing protocols and guidelines that ensure long-term growth for the Web'. Quoted directly from http://www.w3.org/Consortium/ it is an invaluable source of standards and support for web developers and consultants from all over the world and is considered to be the de facto source of information.

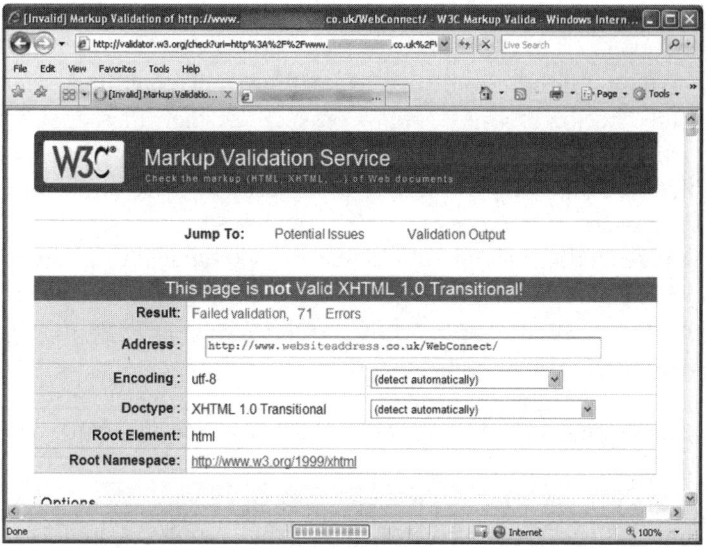

Fig. 13 Failed HTML.

can be very off-putting to say the least. It might as well be in another language and has been known to result in phone conversations to the web developer that can verge on hysterical ("Aaahhh! Why does it say 'failed' on my screen?"). See Fig. 13.

You could also run some online tests for accessibility. Try searching on "accessibility" or "free accessibility tools".

You may not be able to do anything about this yourself but, if you have concerns about whether your website is accessible, you can raise the question with your web developer with a little firepower behind you.

What to do with the results
Don't let any small errors – particularly in links – worry you or reduce your confidence in the developers or designers that you went to so much trouble to find. I have never known a website declared ready for publishing – or already online –

that doesn't have some tiny little thing that needs to be attended to.

These can be errors such as spelling and typos (that your spell checker doesn't find – or such as their/there/they're errors), simple link errors (link to picture 1 actually links to picture 2 and vice versa, easy to do, easy to correct) or more serious errors in process.

I recently encountered such an example in a newly published online directory. It is free to sign up but – in the process of signing up – while trying to access the terms and conditions, you are informed that:

> You are not authorized to view this resource. You need to login.

But you can't log in until you have signed up! We all know (hopefully or at least we do now) that no-one should ever (even though we all do from time to time) sign up to something without reading the terms and conditions; you might be agreeing to pay £1,000 per month, forever.

To be fair to the company running the website, it has agreed that the website will be changed as soon as possible. However, at the time of writing the problem is still there; I wonder how long it might remain.

When you have finished all the checking, give your list of queries to the designers in a matter of fact way. Don't apologize, but certainly don't be upset or angry with them. Make sure you do not pay the final bill until the errors are corrected or you receive satisfactory explanations of how specific things function.

USER TESTING

You should certainly test your website before it is released on unsuspecting users; preferably you should test it a number of times throughout the process.

This may be overkill if you are just having a small website

to profile your business online. However, I would suggest that any website should be tested with real users at two stages: the preliminary design before it is signed off; and definitely the finished or nearly finished product before it goes online.

A larger project – particularly one that is critical to the functioning of the business – will benefit many times over in terms of return on investment (ROI) if tests are carried out at intervals in the development process. User testing often shows up things that neither you as client nor the web developers can see.

As the business owner or similar, you know everything there is to know about the business so can't begin to understand it from the point of view of a user who may know absolutely nothing about the business.

The web developers are likely to have been working on this project on and off for weeks or even months and now feel that they know absolutely everything there is to know about your business (and by now are probably sick of the sight of it – sounds offensive but is the truth; when you design something, you look at it so closely for so long the phrase 'can't see the wood for the trees' might have been written for that very purpose).

User testing can be complex and expensive. Even though all the research and figures show that the ROI in usability testing is very high, the scale of your project may not be large enough to accommodate more than a few pounds to allocate to testing.

However, it is not so hard to get some insights into how it is for real people to use your website by conducting some observed sessions yourself.

How to do some basic user testing
To carry out some user testing you need:

• Some users.

• A computer.

- An internet connection, preferably one that is in common use or a copy of your website on CD. (This will not be so effective as you will not be affected by download times or delays in broadband service.)

- A place to test.

- Hopefully someone to observe while you facilitate, or vice versa.

Who to test with

Some users can be recruited from family or friends or anyone you can persuade to take part. It is better if they meet your target market (as discussed in Chapter 4, Who is the Website for Anyway?).

It is not such a good idea to use employees as they will already know about your business and also are less likely to be honest as they may not want to: a) offend you; b) lose their jobs.

Also, it is not effective to use people who are in the internet or computer business as your test users. They are likely to find it hard simply to use the site, as mentioned previously. They cannot help themselves but become critics and suggest help or improvements.

How many?

Even if you can only find one person who is willing to be your guinea pig, it is better to test with one user than none. Testing with three or four users would be better but any test will show up some problems if they exist. The second, third or fourth tests provide more insights into whether something really is an issue and can be useful to confirm that it definitely is a problem. If you have only tested with one user, it could be that he or she just isn't familiar with something that might be a common feature or convention and may have the same trouble with every website visited.

Testing with three or four users – if conducted properly – will show up most of the problems. In fact, there is evidence that the ROI reduces with each test conducted over five users[3]. With each new test you find out fewer new things and simply confirm the things that you have found before.

What equipment do you need?

You need a computer that is able to access the internet, assuming that the website is already online. Even if it is not 'live', many web designers will put a copy of the site in development in a 'holding area'. This might not be on your domain where it will go eventually, but in some other location. They would then supply a link so that you can view it online as the project progresses. If this is not the case, it is usually possible for them to supply a copy of the website on a CD.

You may want to check this point with the developer at the time of commissioning the website.

Where to test

You need to carry this out in a room where you will not be disturbed or where there are no distractions. This could even be in your or the test user's home; in fact, if it is in the place where the user normally uses the internet, it makes the test conditions particularly authentic.

There is no need to take the authenticity of the test conditions too far. If the user generally accesses the internet in his *open plan* home, do not be tempted to replicate normality by adding a few children doing homework or watching TV and someone setting the table for dinner while moaning about

---

3. Jacob Neilson's Alertbox column of 19/03/2000, Why you only need to test with five users, can be found at http://www.useit.com/alertbox/20000319.html. Even though the document was written several years ago it remains true: the internet changes, people don't.

the dreadful day he has had at work; even if this is close to the user's everyday situation.

Facilitating the testing yourself
All this assumes that you are going to facilitate the test yourself. If you are a sole trader business and cannot afford or persuade anyone else to do it, then it must by default be you.

Take heed that the job of facilitating is not easy for everyone. You need to be a calm communicator type of person, not someone who is quite likely to butt in and try to tell the users how they should be doing it.

If you are a person who, if asked to show someone how to do something on a computer, does not have the patience or attention span and instead of showing them how to do it, just does it for them, then consider trying to get someone else to facilitate while you observe.

There is a bizarre logic in the above behaviour. In principle, if you show people how to do something, they shouldn't need to ask you again. If you don't have the patience to show them and are the type of person who will do it for them instead this can have two outcomes: it can result in either they have to keep asking you forever as they don't know how; or, they have learnt that they don't need to, as they can come to you and you will do it for them; or, if they really did want to know how, next time they ask someone else.

Ensure that the facilitators have read this chapter and the guidelines below (and do stick to them). It can be advantageous for you to observe the testing, but if you do so, ensure that you do not interfere. Facilitating, taking notes and observing are hard to do all at the same time (easier for women, of course, as they are better at multi-tasking!).

Briefing the tester

Before you begin, ensure that you introduce the test situation clearly. It is crucial that the users know:

1. That the test is being carried out so that we can see what the website is like for real people to use.

2. That it is the website that is being tested, not them. They therefore cannot do anything wrong, make mistakes or break anything.

3. That if they have questions we might be able to answer them but because we are trying to be as close as possible to a real situation (where it is unlikely they would have someone sitting alongside to help them) we may not be able to answer until the end of the test (assuming they still want to know at that point). *This is more important than you might immediately give credit for. It is crucial that users are relaxed and uninhibited about conducting the test, and if you simply refuse to answer a question, or remain silent when asked it is likely to remind them of an exam situation, thus changing their state of mind and consequent behaviour.*

4. That they will be asked straightforward questions and asked to carry out straightforward tasks, some might be very prescriptive, others might be more open where they can make their own decisions or choices, just like they would do while on the internet normally.

5. That in order to get the best out of the session, we need to know what is going through their minds at the time of doing something, so it helps us if they will 'think out loud' as they are doing it. You may need to encourage this as you go along; you want them to describe what they are thinking and why they are taking particular actions or paths.

First of all, put the website on the screen and ask them what they think it is (not what they think of it, what type of company they think it is for or what they might be able to do with it). This will show up very quickly if your website satisfies its primary function: do people immediately know where they are and that they are in the right place (if they are looking for your company or what your company provides)?

You can probably ignore their comments about whether they like the colour or whatever; everybody has a different opinion on such things and they can change like the wind. However, if everyone you test makes a comment about the same thing, you should consider discussing this with your designers. You might conclude together that it is appropriate for your industry, or maybe that the sludge brown colour your company has been using since 1953 has to go.

Then ask the users to carry out a series of simple tasks. Do not give the second one until the first one has been carried out; this better mimics how people naturally interact with websites. It is even better if the second task is something that the users carry out naturally.

SAMPLE TASKS
Basic tasks
These are basic requirements, common to most websites:

- Find the telephone number.

- Where is the company located? Find a map to the office.

- How long has the company been in business?

- What types of products or services does the company offer?

Sounds very simplistic, but you may or may not be surprised at the expensive websites where it is impossible to find out these things easily.

Specific tasks
Specific to your website or that mimic real world behaviour:

- Find information about a particular product or service (that you offer and is detailed on your site). For example, how much a set of four teak garden chairs costs and whether matching benches are available.

- Find out about delivery terms and costs.

- Find out what your opening hours are.

- Can a representative, fitter or whatever call to the user's home or office?

- Do you operate an out-of-hours service?

These are suggestions; hopefully you will get the idea from these. It is crucial that the task is something that you would expect your customer to use your website for, and it must actually be possible. Remember we are testing the website, not the users.

Process or transactional tasks
These apply only if your website is more complex and includes e-commerce, online transactions or enquiries on real-time data (such as availability of tickets or stock).

- Find if an item is in stock, how much it is, what colours/sizes/variations it comes in, etc.

- Actually go through the process of buying or booking something, e.g. if you sell tickets to concerts or other events, if you have tickets to a specific artist.

- Search for what concerts are on in their area in the next three months and book one for a party of people.

And more open and natural tasks:

- Find and buy a book that interests the users.

- Research and order suitable flooring/furniture/accessories for their home within a specific budget.

Note: if you ask people to carry out a transaction, you will have to check in advance whether the transaction system is working yet. If it is not, simply stop them at the point where they can go no further and praise them. If it is working, you will need to supply them with your credit card to carry it out. If there is an option in the process that asks if you want to save these details on the computer for future use, make sure they click on NO, or they may find themselves able to make future purchases with your credit card details!

Hopefully you will get the drift from this. Don't make it complicated; you are not trying to catch them out. The important thing is not to interfere. Do not prompt or help them. If someone asks, "What do I do now?" then reply, "What do you think you might try?"

If someone naturally moves onto another task. For example, "Now that I've found the book I'm looking for shall I check on delivery charges?" then go with it. This situation is better as this is nearer to the way someone uses the website in the real world.

Observe and make notes

If you are observing, make sure you keep quiet. Even though it might be hard and at times you might be desperate to help them (or even to shout "JUST CLICK ON THE XXXXX BUTTON FOR GOD'S SAKE") it is important that you are as unobtrusive as possible.

Take notes during the session of anything anyone had

trouble with (especially the points where you wanted to shout at them). It helps if you have a list of the tasks (a copy if you are not facilitating) and can make the notes in conjunction with these. Note not only anything they had trouble with, but also what they actually did at that point and if possible what their 'thinking out loud' told you. This is often where the greatest insights are gained.

How long to test for
You should not keep any individual test user for more than one hour. This would be made up of ten minutes or so to introduce the process and then 30 or 40 minutes in the actual testing, followed by a further five minutes to answer questions and thank them.

Bearing in mind that the normal human attention span is just twenty minutes, then this is long enough. If you prepare your questions and tasks well, you will find it is fairly easy to identify any glaring problems.

Of course, do not expect to be able to find every single thing or to be able to gain insights into complex issues that may be the result of a number of interacting factors. That is the job of a professional and, if your budget allows, you should certainly use a company that provides usability reviews and testing.

Professional usability testing
Usability consultants would carry out testing in a similar way to that which we have just discussed, only in a lot more detail and, of course, with a lot more expertise.

They would be likely to have a purpose-built observation room where you could watch the testing through one-way glass and also see the users' mouse movements on a computer screen (other than the one they are using).

They would also use sophisticated (expensive) software to

record all the mouse movements for future review, probably video the users for their expressions and comments and might possibly have more equipment that tracks their eye-movements. This is all used for analysis and confirmation purposes; it can be hard to take all the small incidents in at once and looking back over a recording of a user test often allows the identification of critical minutiae that might otherwise be missed.

Professional usability reviews

A review is where experts in website usability identify problems with the website from their knowledge of principles and conventions. They also carry out what are termed 'cognitive walkthroughs' for parts of the website that might involve a process, such as an online purchase or enquiry process.

The reviewers put themselves in the position of the users and go through the process step-by-step, noting where there may be problems, confusion, ambiguities, etc.

The feedback from these sessions is often provided to you in the form of a written report, although it can be more useful (and sometimes cheaper) to forego a fat report for some time spent with the consultants going through and discussing the problems with you. They should also be able to advise on prioritizing your and your web developers' efforts on fixing the things that are most important.

Get the web designers or developers to observe

If you carry out user testing, the best scenario is if the web designers or developers can actually observe. If the process of facilitating is completely new to you maybe you should invite them in to see the second user test. This will allow you a chance to get the process sorted out and they won't be huffing and puffing with impatience in the background while you break out into a sweat because you can't get online or whatever. If you commission professional testing, you should insist they attend and observe. It can save a multitude of arguments about what they think 'might happen' or how the users 'might interact' with the site. There is no substitute for evidence that occurs before your very eyes.

Discuss straightaway

Discuss the things you have observed as soon as possible after the testing; they are then fresh in your mind. Even the following day you will have forgotten a lot of the detail.

Record the outcomes. Then work with the web developers to prioritize any changes. It is not practical or desirable to change every tiny thing that may show up. Give first priority to things that are easy to change and don't take much time; then to things which are crucial to the functioning of the site, and to things that prevent the user getting it in the first instance.

Remember that the reason for all this work is the hard fact that there is no point whatsoever in getting people to your website through SEO, adwords or any other strategy if, when they arrive at your website, they look around in bewilderment for a few seconds and then click on the back button, or if the very thing you want them to do (to buy something or make an enquiry for example) is too difficult or even impossible to accomplish.

Extra work?

Unless the website is completely finished and published, the designers should not treat any of this as extra work, provided that you informed them at the outset of the project that there was going to be testing as mentioned above.

Of course, we would hope that there are no problems at all, although in practice, even with the most experienced of designers, this is relatively unlikely.

TESTING FOR SEARCH ENGINE OPTIMIZATION
We also need to test the website to see if all our Search Engine Optimization efforts are paying off. In other words, can the search engines find it?

Optimization testing
The purpose of testing in this case is a crucial stage. Quite simply, the optimization testing of a website is something that all website owners should do to establish whether they have an effective website in the search engines.

It is obvious to most that if we positioned a shop (an actual shop, not a website) hidden down a side road or in a lane behind the high street, where hardly anyone ever walks as it doesn't 'go' anywhere, that shop will not have the same business turnover as a similar shop that is in the centre of town, in the high street, or on the main thorough-fare.

In many large cities, as you walk along the main shopping centres it is common to see people with 'sandwich-boards' or holding up other signs pointing to the side- or back-street businesses.

These are the search engines of the real world helping the shopkeeper get more business and the shoppers find the shop they are looking for. The same sort of thing has to be done on the internet; we have to ensure that the shopper or customer can find the site. To see how effective this is, we have to test your sign, in other words, test the optimization of your website.

Key phrases
Testing the key phrases to see if the results page brings your site to the first ten positions is the only definitive way of declaring a success. Do the main search engines have your details? What do these details say about your site? Can your

website statistics (log files) give you any further information on the traffic you already get?

I was discussing with a client – quite a few years ago – about how to improve the marketing of his business when the subject of the internet arose. He said, "Don't talk to me about the internet, I've had a website for four years and never had a single enquiry from it."

Some very simple testing showed that he did not have any contact details on the site and the site was not registered with any of the search engines.

When I returned six months later, after carrying out an internet marketing project using a selection of the techniques detailed in this book, the story was quite different.

Within six months he was listed in the search engine results pages at number one for two of the most valuable key phrases in his industry and he has remained there for five years, all for a small consultancy fee.

The moral of this story is that testing for search engine optimization is an easy process and applies to an established website as well as a newly published or redeveloped one.

Google testing facilities
As Google is the market leader for search in the UK (some 68 per cent of people use Google in the UK), it makes sense that you do these tests using the Google search facilities. They are free and easy to use:

- Open up your browser (Internet Explorer or similar) and go to the Google website by entering www.google.co.uk into the address bar.

- In the search box (text entry box) enter the following 'info: your website address'.

- Press the return or enter key and you will be presented with a screen that will provide information about your site (or the site you are testing).

The details shown should be familiar to you as you will have written or entered this text into your website. It shows what Google will present about that page of your website in the search results.

Look at the title and description and check to see if it is communicating the message that you want in the search results. If you have done your optimization correctly, this should be the title you put into your site and the description should be the one you assigned to the web page being tested.

Google's cache

This is the picture and information that Google has about a website. It will show the information that Google cached the last time it visited the site.

Unless you update your site many times per day which will result in Google visiting your site more often, Google is likely to visit your site every 28 days. This means that when you check Google's cache the information you see could be up to 28 days old (or might be the information from yesterday). If you update your site often (like many news or current affairs websites), Google might visit your site daily, thus the information might be current or no more than 24 hours old.

Find web pages similar to yours

The websites listed here will probably be competitor sites and will be listed in the same section of the Google directory.

If you go through the same process on these sites you will find that they have your site listed in their 'similar to' list.

Find web pages that link to your site (referral listings)

This is an important piece of information. This shows how many websites are linked to your site and which ones they are.

Look through these results and click through to the sites to see if you are aware of these incoming links. They may be sites you do not want a link from or you may not want your business to be associated with. If so, contact them directly and request that the link is removed.

Find web pages from the site (search engine listing)

This shows all the pages of your website that Google has registered.

This information allows you to find out if Google has missed any of the pages in your site. If there are important pages that have been missed you need to ensure that they are added. If you do this, you will need to return at a later date and repeat this process to see if Google has picked up the missing pages.

Find web pages that contain the term (referral listings)

This will show the websites that Google has found that have a reference to your website.

As above, it is important that you look through these links and go to the websites that are linking in to your website. Using this you can discover what is published online about you, what has been written about you or how you are described elsewhere.

If anyone has written anything defamatory or there are items that are not complimentary to your business, you will at least be informed of them and have the opportunity to take relevant action to remove this information.

This results page will also provide the opportunity to see if your site has been listed in the directories you have subscribed to.

BENCHMARK TESTING

In order to measure any kind of change or progress, we must first identify and record the starting point, state or condition. Then, when the end point, result or outcome is reached, we can make a comparison between the two.

This also applies to the internet. How do you know how far you have moved if you do not know where you started from?

The benchmark test is the only way to establish a start point for your website; this must be carried out before any optimization is carried out. It will help to give you a picture of what your website performance is like before any activities including optimization so you can identify improvements as a result of the project.

The most efficient way to benchmark your website and one of the easiest ways to find out what is happening with your website is to make use of your website statistics.

Website statistics

One of the most important stages of any marketing process is gathering and interpreting feedback.

There is a saying in the marketing world: "Fifty per cent of all advertising works. If only we knew which fifty per cent".

Interestingly, using the website statistics we can actually see what kind of actions work and what doesn't. In order to do this, we need to benchmark the website's performance. The statistics of your website can be studied every day for you to establish trends and visitor usage.

Every web hosting company should be able to offer you access to statistical data and analyses of your website activities. In fact we always recommend that if they cannot, or refuse to, you should find a new hosting company.

The statistics consist of a software application that is installed on the web server (computer) on which your website is hosted, the hosting company then allow you password access to the information. This does not usually require any special skills and certainly no knowledge of statistics.

There are many programs available for website hosting companies to provide this service, for example: Aw stats; Webalizer; Matrix Stats; to name but a few. As they are server based packages, some hosting services offer them for free, others may make a charge.

There are other analytical programs available which give you more detailed information but these can cost a considerable amount of money. For the small business website, the programs I have mentioned above will give sufficient information for basic analysis.

The kind of information you are looking for includes the:

- Number of visitors.

- Entry pages.

- Exit pages.

- Referring search engines.

- Referring websites.

- Search terms used by the visitor from the search engines.

There are many other sets of information with these website analysis programs such as country of origin and time spent on the site.

Ranking check
Put simply, the ranking is the position in the search engine results for a given key phrase. This is what Search Engine Optimization (SEO) is all about!

If you have researched and carried out the optimization processes correctly, you should have a fairly high ranking for the key phrase you have assigned for a given web page.

It is important that you establish the ranking of your web

224 Testing Testing Testing

page before the optimization process begins so that you have a benchmark, a datum point with which to compare future results. Any better ranking after this will show the improvement that the optimization has brought to the page. After the optimization allow a period of six weeks and then carry out the test again to see if there has been any improvement.

This test should be repeated every month to check the current position and also after any other promotional techniques are applied to the site. Following optimization, you should see a steady improvement of the ranking of your web page; it will obviously peak at some point – we hope at number one.

Carrying out ranking checks
This can either be carried out manually, or software can be purchased to carry out the ranking check for you.

The manual check is for those who have time on their hands. Like other testing procedures it is easy but tedious. Type in the search term (the key phrase for that page) and then look through the search engines' results for your web page.

If you do this often and do not have the time to scroll through hundreds of search pages for your website, you might consider the purchase of a software program to carry out this function.

The software can do your work whilst you get on with something else. It can review many more pages and more search engines and save you a great deal of time. Whilst this information is presented in report form, the interpretation and development of keyword strategies remains the skill of the expert and like other processes you should not rely on a piece of software to do the work for you. The users of your site are human and do not conform to computer predictions.

Whichever method you use, it is important for you to carry

out this activity on a regular basis. The shortest period that we have succeeded in improving the ranking is six days from no listing in the first 100 pages to number two on page one.

Link check

Links are important for the site to get high ranking. These are links from other websites into your site. The most important ones are high ranking websites; examples of high ranking websites are dependent on the search or key phrase but common examples would include the BBC, government sites, those that get very high numbers of visitors consistently such as Amazon.

We have already seen the information available in Google on links to your site; of course, this only includes the links that Google has listed.

To get a link popularity report for all the major search engines, there are a number of tools available on the internet.

Various online services can perform a link check for you. One of these: 'Link popularity' can be found online at http://www.linkpopularity.com. It just requires your website address to access an online report.

Type in your website home page address and the software will do the rest. The report will show you how many links each search engine has for your site. If you want your own copy of the report, you will have to supply an email address to them.

You can also download free software to carry out link checks. One example is available at http://www.check yourlinkpopularity.com. Like most free software found online this is a 'light' version with limited functionality. The full version is available for a fee.

Note: If you decide to supply an email address to a free service in order to get a report or similar, consider using a 'disposable' email address. Set up an address in Yahoo or some other free service. They will probably conduct a check that the email address you supply is a valid one and it is quite likely that the address will receive a lot of spam in the future.

Ongoing testing

The search engines are always making adjustments to their search and ranking criteria; if you do not keep an eye on your site listings, you could drop off the screen without knowing about it.

You may get an indication when the enquiries fall off or when the phone stops ringing but this is too late.

Optimization tests should be repeated every few weeks to ensure that the site ranking remains high. It is a way of finding out if the promotional activities that you are carrying out are being effective.

14

PUBLISH AND PROMOTE

I recently went to visit a potential new client to talk about the promotion of his website. When I went into the office I noticed that there were numerous boxes stacked up around the room and under the desk.

After general introductions and so on, the new client reached down under his desk and pulled something out of one of the boxes. "Have one of our brochures," he said, handing a lovely, glossy, expensive-looking document to me. "Thank you," I said and while turning the pages enquired as to when this had been produced. "Oh, last year," was the reply, "And how many did you have printed?" I asked, realizing from his answer that it looked as though most of them were still here. Were they for an event, an exhibition or something I wondered, why were they still under the desk?

It turned out that they were general brochures and were planned for general use. There were so many because it was cheaper to have a large number printed at once. They contained a lot of detail including prices – which meant that they were likely to go out of date in a fairly short time.

"If they are under your desk then no potential customers can see them," I pointed out, "So it doesn't matter how cheap they were, they may as well not have been printed, if no-one is going to be reading them." I couldn't help but feel sorry for him as he realized that he had wasted a lot of money and that the effort of getting them to potential customers was going to take a lot of time and possibly be more expensive than getting them printed in the first place.

If you commission a website, publish it onto the internet and then do absolutely no promotion, you may as well have the boxes of brochures sitting under *your* desk. Your website will become nothing more than an expensive virtual doorstop unless you make some kind of effort to reach your market and enable your potential customers to find it.

Even before the website is published, plans for promotion should be drawn up so that the best possible outcome from your investment can be made. Start with an outline action plan. As with any other business activity, if you have an overview of what is going to be carried out, you will find it easier to implement.

The publication of a website online is just the beginning of the process of promoting your business online. It is the starting point of a never-ending business activity, not the end of a project.

Publish the site
The final stage is to ensure that the website is complete and ready for publishing online. As detailed in the previous chapter, this should include testing, for the functionality, checking the content and to see if it is easy to use. Once any problems have been ironed out, then the site can be published.

The actual process of publishing a website is not complex and often it is as simple as clicking a button and entering a password. This would normally be carried out by your web designers, or if you are entering or maintaining the content yourself this would be the final action in the process each time you enter or change content.

Earlier days of the internet saw many companies having launch parties and events when they published their website. This has become a less prominent practice unless it coincides with some other promotional activity.

Getting into the search engines

Search engines trawl the internet every minute of every hour of every day looking for new websites to list and to refresh the information on the sites they already have listed. They achieve this by the use of automated programs called robots and spiders.

Do not rely on your web designers or developers to automatically submit your new site to the search engines unless it has been specified in the web design brief and contract. I encounter websites on a regular basis that have vast amounts of data and relevant information on their subjects that are not included in search results because the process of registration has not been carried out. The only reason I have come across them is because their owners have asked me to look into the reasons why they do not get any response from their websites.

Another important factor is the inbound links. These are links from other websites into yours. These connections allow the robots and spiders to follow the links and find your website. If your site does not have any connection with any other site through an inbound link, the website will never be found or automatically listed in any search engine.

So the process of getting into search engines follows two paths: search engine registration and link building (the process of building up inbound links).

Search engine registration

The choice and method of registration of your website with search engines is dependent on which search engines your potential customers use. At the time of writing (for the UK market), the most popular search engine is Google representing approximately 70 per cent of UK users, followed by Yahoo, MSN and Ask. It is worth noting that AOL and Ask use the Google database for their results. This means that your website address inclusion in Google will show up in AOL and Ask searches to a certain degree. However, since both these search engines use different criteria for listing their results, it is important to register in both these sites as well as Google. You must include search engines other than Google to ensure you get the best possible results.

There are hundreds of other search engines on the internet and it will be beneficial to be registered with many of them. Each submission process takes a few minutes to complete so the more you are registering with, the more time you need to allow to complete the process. Ensure that you keep a record of each search engine you have submitted to; you do not want to do this twice.

The first part of this process is to find the search engine submission page. The location of this differs according to the individual search engine. The Google AddURL page is shown in Fig. 14.

The whereabouts of the search engine submission page may be obvious from the home page, but may take a little more effort to find. One way to find the page is to search (within the search engine). In the search box, try entering 'add URL', 'add website', 'submit website', or 'website submission'. One of these should indicate the page you need in the search results.

Note that all the major search engines have country specific websites so it is important that you submit to the UK version of the search engine. If you are using the search to find the submission page, do a UK search only. If not, you may find the global or .com submission page by accident.

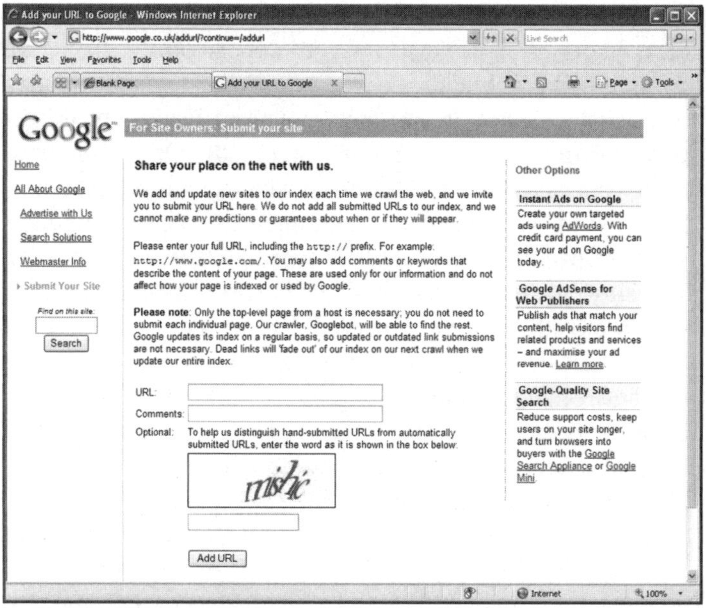

Fig. 14 Google's AddURL page.

Google has one of the simplest submission pages as they only require the website address of the index or home page. Make sure you include the http:// before your website address so the address looks like http://www.mycompanywebsitename.co.uk. They also ask for comments. These should be essential keywords and phrases for the site. This will ensure that your site is included in the correct part of their database so, when someone looks for your type of service or product, the Google search engine can find the information quickly.

It can take up to two months to get registered in a search engine using this method. Allow four to six weeks after submission and then check to see if your site is included in the search engine. This is easily achieved by conducting a search for your website in that search engine: simply type your complete website address in the search field of the site and look for your site in the results. Bear in mind that your site is likely, though not certain, to appear on the first page for your exact web address. The process of registration may need to be repeated if you have not been listed, but do not do this activity more than once a month. Once you have found your site, stop submitting to that search engine.

A word of warning, there are numerous software products available to register your site automatically, all of them promising to save you time and effort. As submission via these is not often favoured by search engines, their use can be risky. Extensive use of these software programs has prompted search engine companies to develop systems to prevent these software programs from using their submission forms. You may notice when submitting your site that the search engine submission forms have a security code which you have to enter when you submit your site. Google is one of the sites that offers both manual and automated options. However, in my experience, they are slower at listing a site in their database that has been submitted by software than one that has been submitted manually.

You can fast track submission with some of the search engines although this usually incurs a fee. Some search engines such as Yahoo have an express submission service for an annual fee.

If your business has a wide geographical scope or you want to promote your business in another country, there are a number of considerations. Many country specific search engines will not allow your site to be listed unless you are based in that country. Others will only permit inclusion if the site is in that country's language. Check these things out before you waste time trying to register your website.

When you go through the search engine submission process, they will usually request an email address. This is to send a confirmation but also often results in spam. As explained in the last chapter, to avoid unnecessary spam it is a good idea to set up a temporary or 'disposable' email address for this purpose. Create a new email address with Hotmail, Gmail or Yahoo and use this address for your submissions. Any spam will then go to this account, avoiding your own business mailbox.

Building an inbound links list

Search engines, especially Google, use the links to your site from other websites to give ranking or score to your site. The more links you have, the higher the ranking, the higher your site will appear in the results pages. Not all links carry the same value however, some have a higher rating than others. For example, large or highly visited sites like the BBC or Government websites carry a high importance, while some links – specifically from link farms (websites that exist only to make links going to multiple websites) may even reduce your rank. Due diligence must be carried out on the sites that link to you so you only gain from this enhancement technique.

Google offer a browser toolbar that includes a rank check facility. It is worth downloading this and using it for the duration of the link building process. Each time you visit a website the toolbar will display Google's rank for that site; the higher the rank, the more valuable a link from that site to yours will be. Spend some time working on who should link to you. Start with your suppliers; these are in a vertical market giving relevance to your business. Most suppliers will be happy to list you on their website as, for example, it gives their customers a local contact for the purchase of products they make. If you are a business to business company, look at your customers and evaluate them for link building. Further links can be identified from other activities that are mentioned in subsequent sections of this chapter.

Register with directories

As the search engines are becoming much more effective in returning relevant results for local searches, directories that have previously specialized in local listings such as Yell, Thompson Local and many others may begin to lose their market share.

There are hundreds or even thousands of regional or industry specific as well as general web directories on the internet. Each one seems to be saying, "We can get you more business if you buy our enhanced listing package," or words to that effect. If you decide to invest your hard earned marketing budget, are you likely to get enough extra business to justify the cost?

Initially most online directories gave listings away for free. This was to encourage businesses to submit their details in order to grow the directories' databases. The online directory needs a critical mass of listings – the principle that 'size matters' is a common one in the internet world – so that there will be a variety of results for most enquiries, users and researchers will find what they are looking for and therefore use the directory again as well as recommending it to others.

A growing number of online directories have started charging for your entry in their database. Whilst some basic listings remain free, many now charge a single one-off payment of maybe a few pounds or dollars and to encourage you to spend a little more they offer 'enhanced' listings.

Basic listings often do not include a link to your website; some do not even provide a contact number. These are obviously of limited use to a business as in order to be found or contacted the user or researcher would need to use a search engine (or another directory) to find your company. This takes more time and, of course, they are only then likely to find you if you have an optimized website (but that is another story).

If you have registered on a local directory, sooner or later you will probably get a call from them – a soft and persuasive voice on the phone expressing the importance of having an enhanced listing. Initially resolute, you weaken and, before you know it, you give your credit card details to them. The telesales operative assures you of greater exposure for your business and many more enquiries from your enhanced listing at the top of the page! You certainly don't want to be buried in the mass of free basic listings do you?

The initial warm fuzzy feeling and vision of lots of new enquiries may soon give way to doubts: Is this value for money? Will I get the return that is implied? Have I spent wisely?

Like anything in life, 'you pay your money and take your chance'; and like any business investment – however small – it is prudent to carry out appropriate research before committing to any expenditure, considering potential ROI and how focused or targeted this opportunity is, ultimately: how will it serve your business?

During my research I have looked in some detail into the issues surrounding directory registration and enhanced listings. Having researched what is on offer from sixteen major web directories in the UK, the results have been quite startling. From the data collected and analysed I have put together a few tips to make the decision process a little more specific.

Check the listing status of the directory in Google, Yahoo and MSN. Type the directory website address (URL) into the search field (info:www.directoryname.com) and see how many results are returned. The following checks can be found – number of web pages that contain the URL, the number of links into the site from other sites and the number of links from the site. The higher the number of links into the site, the better the directory is doing from a search engine and online promotion perspective.

Contact companies who have already paid for an enhanced listing (you should be able to get their contact details from their enhanced listing!) and ask them if it has resulted in more business. It is better to look at companies in your own sector to get a clearer understanding of what is happening. People may use the directories for builders or financial advisers but not for engineering or consultancy.

Ask the directory owners for information on the number of visitors to the site each day, the number of searches done on the site each day and how many registered users they have. What methods are they using to promote the site online and offline? This is called a press pack in the industry and is normal for any advertising media; you need to ask for it and study it carefully when it arrives. There should be evidence that the statistics provided are carried out by an independent third party in order to demonstrate unbiased claims. ABCE (http://www.abce.org.uk) are the official body and are a subsidiary of the Audit Bureau of Circulation (ABC). They set the standards!

As well as comparing visitor numbers and other figures, compare the prices charged for the enhanced listing with other directories. Which one is likely to give the best bang for your buck?

Does the directory require users to log in to access the database? Many do this in order to collect email addresses which are then valuable for marketing purposes or can be a valuable asset if sold on to third parties. Not only does this present a barrier to users, it also causes problems with search engines. Robots that create the listings are not going to be able to access the data and only those who are registered will see your advertisement.

These simple checks will allow you to make a far more informed judgement on where you should consider spending your advertising budget. Do the checks and, if you decide to pay for an enhanced listing, you know you are spending your budget wisely.

ONLINE PR
Press releases

All new activities such as product launches, new employees and big contracts for business should be profiled with a press release. This is a way of notifying the wider audience of the developments within your business. You can employ the services of a PR agency or if you have the writing skills and understand the format required, it is possible to author the press statements and release them through PR distribution services on the internet.

Many websites that provide this service are available online and will display your business news. The free services will only distribute to a small number of outlets and a fee is usually required for your press release to reach a wider journalistic audience. A vast quantity of press releases are distributed each day so your article must stand out. Providing relevant photographs or video to enhance the story can help, but only if they are good quality (unless you really have some crucial breaking news in which case video taken on a mobile phone held out of the window of a moving car will make the main news broadcasts). If the press release is of merit, the distribution and take up from journalists can be considerable.

Articles

These can increase the credibility of your business if your industry is based on knowledge of some kind. It is important that, like press releases, they are not sales pitches and contribute knowledge rather than just blow your trumpet. However, before embarking on this route ensure that you really can write and that you know what you are talking about. Any facts must be verified as any inaccuracies will be found out. This can do more damage than good for your business if you are not up to the job.

Most sites that accept articles, such as news and article

submission sites (which can easily be found by searching) require between 250 and 800 words depending where you post them. Be aware that it is very common for your article to be stolen and used by another site or passed off as someone else's work. You cannot prevent this but if you include some unique phrase or error (an anagram or your nickname or similar) it can help you to identify your work and prove it is yours.

Forum boards

A forum is a type of website or area in a website where users can post questions and responses, or enter into discussion and debate usually on specialized subjects. In Chapter 4, Who is the Website for Anyway?, we examined in some detail the process of defining your target customer. From the investigations and analysis we should have a reasonably clear picture of where our target customers may be found online – in particular which forum boards they might use to seek information on their subject.

It is an interesting phenomenon of human nature that people have a desire to interact with others; to help others; or sometimes to compete by demonstrating their superior knowledge. We can sometimes take advantage of this by posing pertinent questions on forum boards encouraging a response from others, while highlighting our product or service.

A software development company wanted to promote its new software online. I had spent some time optimizing the site which was starting to produce results. Unfortunately, this was not getting as much response as they wanted, mostly because there was no generic name for the type of software they were selling. One large target market was small independent accountants many of which were members of a large online community website for their profession. I posted a request for information on the type of software the company supplied. Within a few days there were a number of responses recommending various software packages that could do the same or similar to my clients. I instructed the client to post a response to my question offering their software explaining their product. This gave them the opportunity to be seen by their target market; the question posed may have alerted a number of potential customers to whom it had not occurred that this type of software was useful to them.

Their sales went up by 400 per cent over the following weeks. The owners of the forum board wrote an article on the different software packages that were available, and in the reviews my client's package came out top for its simplicity. In addition, we were able to create a link from the forum board to their site, thus increasing their ranking.

When a link is created to your site, it can take a number of forms. The most common is to see your company name *mycompany* or website address www.mycompany.co.uk with the words representing a link to the website. Other options are a link from a picture or logo, but the most useful in terms of ranking is a keyword link, where the keywords or a description of the product are coded to become a link to the website. Links from respected forum boards often have a high ranking so linking in this method is particularly useful.

Beware, however, as this approach must be subtly undertaken. Most forum boards do not allow advertising, so the method of asking a question (which is actually a request for the product), then responding to this by embedding a word link must be seen as a convenience for the questioner, not as a blatant sales pitch.

Blogs
Short for Weblog a blog is like an online personal diary. People use them for many purposes, including keeping

friends or colleagues updated on travel or activities to sounding off about topical issues.

In the last few years the use of blogs has greatly enhanced the opportunities for search engine rank improvements. A considerable amount of thought should be given to the writing of a blog as they are demanding of time and resources. If you follow any blogs online you will see that many of them are updated infrequently and are often dropped after a few months when the commentary runs out. In the same manner as forum boards, responses to blogs can be employed to embed links to your website.

Email promotion

Do your current customers know what the full range of your products and services are? The only way to be sure is to tell them! You can go to the expense and time to develop a brochure, have it printed and then send it out in the post for them to throw it in the bin. Alternatively, you can develop an email campaign and email all of your customers at the same time. This is more immediate and will be considerably cheaper than a brochure.

Before you embark on developing an email marketing strategy and campaign, think carefully about how much you hate the time-wasting of responding to spam. As you are going to be sending out advertising, it is essential to comply with the law: the privacy and electronic communications (EC directive) regulations 2003[1], the Committee of Advertising Practice (CAP) code – the rules set by the advertising standards authority (ASA).[2] Other legal requirements include (as with your website), that if you are a limited company, a charity or a limited partnership (and registered with Companies House) you must include your

---

1. Details on www.opsi.gov.uk.
2. Information can be found on this at http://www.asa.org.uk.

registered address and your company registration number in any email correspondence. This has been a requirement since January 2007. This serves an additional purpose in that you comply with the legislation and it gives credibility to your email if the recipient sees that the email is from a bonafide business (which can be traced through an organization such as Companies House). If in any doubt whatsoever, you should seek qualified legal advice before proceeding.

All promotional emails from one offs to newsletters must have an 'opt out' or unsubscribe. This serves two purposes. It complies with the Code of Advertising Practice and it reduces the chance that your email address ends up in a black list or spam folder in your recipient's computer. The simpler the unsubscribe process, the better. A simple link at the top and bottom of the email, which opens the client email browser and completes the subject line, will make it more preferable for the recipient to use than the possibility of entering your email address into the black list.

How often should you send a promotional email or newsletter to your clients is a question I often get asked at seminars. It depends on the size of your company, the nature of your products and a host of other things. Like all aspects of business, set your objectives and expected outcomes for each email and develop the strategy to achieve this.

Each time you send out a promotional email you need to create content which uses up time and effort. This can put huge demand on your resources and it can soon be too demanding to maintain and so the campaign will tend to taper off. If you have a team of writers to generate copy for each letter, this is not a problem. If these resources are not available to you, consider only sending a promotional email out every few months.

Another thing to consider is the volume of emails you send out at a time. Do you have the manpower to deal with 20 or 30 enquiries in a day? With response rates of 2 to 3 per cent this equates to 1,000 emails per posting. If the email is crafted well, you can hope for a higher response rate. Be careful with this. One of the things that can destroy a small business very easily is overtrading or trading beyond its capacity. It's not just the fact that you have only one telephone line and are busy on the phone with one client so that anyone else phoning cannot get through, but do you have the stock, or the working capital to acquire the stock to satisfy demand? Some recipients may take a few days to respond but the majority of interested clients will get in touch soon after they receive the email, especially if the offer is time limited. Only send out what you can deal with and monitor it carefully.

Writing the email
I receive (and sometimes read) hundreds of promotional emails on a daily basis. The content is often poor and I find it hard at times to maintain my attention or interest. The communication rarely excites me so I am pleased to delete it and move on to another email where I find similar uninspiring dialogue. This is repeated again and again.

What so many fail to realize is that their customers have little time to spend reading an email unless they perceive – in the first few seconds – that it can benefit them or their business in some way.

How do you get your client to open the email and read the first line? So many emails are deleted without being read because the subject line is uninspiring. Or because the recipient suspects it is spam. This is the part that has to attract attention so the client opens the email. There are many theories on this subject depending on whose book you read or which seminar or training course you attend. Whichever method you use, it should be honest and to the point. Don't be cryptic; try to 'say what it does on the tin' (in the subject line). If you have to read the article to get an explanation of the title it rarely succeeds.

When selecting your Sunday newspaper, what is it that makes you purchase one paper over another? More than likely it is because it is the paper that you would normally buy. What would make you change or buy another in addition to your usual? It may be an offer of a free DVD or the headline that attracts or grabs your attention. Getting the readers' attention is the first and crucial part of a four step process.

Sales communication guidelines

AIDA is a fundamental in promotional and sales communications. Developed in the 1950s and used ever since in a sales context, it has become an essential aspect of all online promotional communication, from the content of promotional emails to press releases, articles and your website.

AIDA is an acronym for:

- **A**ttention: the heading or hook to catch your reader.

- **I**nterest: the first paragraph, short with implications of the rest of the communication.

- **D**esire: the section of the communication that results in the reader wanting more.

- **A**ction: the activity the reader has to take to satisfy his or her desire.

Who is the email for?

Who you send your promotional emails to falls into three categories:

- The subscriber (who has signed up to receive your email).

- The past or existing customer or client.

- The potential customer.

Each one of these needs a different approach in the writing, content and construction of the email.

The subject line
The subject line can vary according to who is to receive it, but all must be assured that it is from a trusted source.

Subscribers will need to recognize something they have signed up for and will open an email newsletter from a website they know they have subscribed to. These email subject lines should mention the newsletter name such as *my company newsletter*. Using a subject line such as this also draws attention to the item in the recipient's email inbox.

Past customers will also require the same assurance so the company name should be included such as *my company website promotion offer*.

Potential customers will need a slightly different approach as they may not have heard of the name of your company so you will need to consider how you can inspire their interest with a relevant subject line. The use of terms such as *increase your profits* or *your business loan is ready* or *job opportunity no investment required* now usually results in instant blacklisting and deletion. These terms have been so over used by spammers that they have lost their effectiveness and should be avoided at all times.

One effective subject line I have used on a number of occasions when promoting a seminar is: Website promotion seminar from (the name of my consultancy business) in (Local town). It is plain and simple and contains lots of real information (what, who, where). In addition, if anyone wants to look up the company online they can do so quite easily and find out more before even opening the email.

The content

Again the content needs to be adjusted to accommodate the type of recipient. When you are writing content try to keep in your head the situation the readers are in. Do they know who you are? Have they signed up to something? Or is this the first time they might have encountered your business? What do they need to know to gain their interest and to be assured that it can be trusted?

For sponsored and past customers the email should always start with the recipient's name. This recognizes that they are known to your business and you care enough about them to address them individually. Invite them to contact you to make any necessary corrections to their personal details. If you are requested to make a change *do so* and do it before the next email goes out. I have been receiving email and information in the post from an organization whose events I go to occasionally. They have spelt my name wrong for years and I have informed them of this on so many occasions I have given up. This has, of course, reduced my confidence in them as an organization and, while I sometimes go to their events, I would be very unlikely to ask them to organize an event for me.

With potential clients it is better to use their name in the email but many email addresses start with info@, ask@, or some other general term. If the email address in your database starts with sales@, try to find another email address for that company. Think about it. The sales department is in the business of selling not buying. They are more likely to delete your email than pass it on to the relevant person in the business who might be interested in your product or service. There are exceptions to this. For example, if you offer sales training it should also be directed to the personnel or Human Resources (HR) department.

Once you have convinced them to open the email, the next part of the content should aim to grab their attention and generate their interest. Think about what would interest you if you were receiving the email.

Move on from the interest to the desire. This is the time to list benefits and use persuasion. Keep the communication short and snappy; all real information, there is no room for waffle or marketing-speak here.

Then don't forget the action. This is the one part of the process that so many company owners fail to include in their promotional correspondence. What prompts would encourage *you* to respond, to pick up the phone or go to the website. Use links to make the process of going to the website easier; there they can find out more about you as a company. It will also help to increase the visitors to the site where you may have other opportunities to attract their attention.

Avoid pictures and images if you can; they may look good but email programs are often set to block images when the software is set up. Unless you absolutely need the email to have an image in it to illustrate a product or similar, avoid it. So no pretties and no gratuitous graphics. Get down to the message.

It is important to monitor traffic to your website from your email campaign. This will give you the opportunity to see how effective your promotional message is. Keep records of any increases in visitor numbers to your website following an email campaign. This can be compared to the same time in a previous week.

Email transmission services
To avoid the problems of junk mail filtering, consider using an email distribution service. While you will have to pay for this service, they can provide monitoring and response services. Also, it is their email address that will end up in a spam filter not yours (so your emails will not be blocked in the future). There are a large number of service providers in the marketplace who can undertake this for you. The usual due diligence should be used when contracting the service.

Promoting the website is an ongoing process which requires a strategic approach. Dealt with carefully it can produce excellent results for your business and bottom line.

AFTERWORD

You have taken positive action to improve your website, to get a website that works for your business or to improve the websites that you work with by buying this book. I hope that you use the knowledge and make a difference. There are millions of websites out there that are not doing this, so even this simple step puts you ahead.

Even if you only implement a few of the ideas and protocols that I have mentioned it will have a positive outcome to your results. I often receive emails from business owners who have attended one of my seminars saying that they had made a few of the changes I recommend and it has made a huge difference to their website.

I hope that by sharing my observations and experiences from all the work that I have carried out over the last ten years it will help you to develop a website that can compete with those organizations out there that have much bigger budgets to pay for expert help.

If you want more support, we run seminars and training workshops all over the UK and beyond. Look us up on the internet or go straight to our website at www.businessfor business.co.uk.

Please let me know what difference it has made to your website and business.[1]

Good luck.

Nigel T. Packer

---

1. Please let me know via my website at www.businessforbusiness.co.uk; we will post a selection of comments there.

INDEX

Index 255

'stop' words   110–111
strapline   186

T

tabbed browsing   123, 124
tagline   186, 187
target market   140–141
telephone numbers   125
templates   157
terminology   82–83
testing the website   196–226
  professional   215–216
  user   206–215
text   52–53, 130
  highlighting   195
  illegible/small   25, 33
  size   33
  underlining   194
title   103, 104
title bar   103
tower ads   57

U

underlined text   194
Unique Selling Points (USPs)   96
updating the website   22, 142,
    176, 177, 183
uploading   59
URL   51
usability consultants   215–216

V

video   53

video streaming   53
viruses   33
visitors to website   38

W

web browsers   202
web feed   60
webbot   57
website
  address   51, 118–120
  content   52, 130, 139–140
  definition of   50
  design   153–154
  design brief   134–146, 180
    process for   180–183
  designers/developers   51–52
    female   161
    finding   148–165
    meeting   163–164
    references   161–162
    shortlist of   162–163
    style of   160–161
    website of   157–158
  pages   50
  promotion   228–247
  rating   121
  readability   189–190
  server   28, 52
  statistics   38, 52, 222–223
  testing   196–226
webstats   52
welcome pages   24, 25–26, 144,
    186
wikis   60
World Wide Web Consortium
    204

To order these Right Way titles please fill in the form below

No. of copies	Title	Price	Total
	Going Self Employed	£5.99	
	The Right Way to Start Your Business	£4.99	
	For P&P add £2.50 for the first book, £1 for each additional book		
	Grand Total		£

Name: _____

Address:_____

_____ Postcode: _____

Daytime Tel. No./Email _____
(in case of query)

Three ways to pay:
1. Telephone the TBS order line on 01206 255 800.
   Order lines are open Monday – Friday, 8:30am–5:30pm.
2. I enclose a cheque made payable to **TBS Ltd** for £_____
3. Please charge my   ☐ Visa   ☐ Mastercard   ☐ Amex
   ☐ Maestro (issue no. _____)

Card number:_____

Expiry date: _____ Last three digits on back of card:_____

Signature: _____

(your signature is essential when paying by credit or debit card)

Please return forms to Cash Sales/Direct Mail Dept.,
The Book Service, Colchester Road, Frating Green,
Colchester CO7 7DW.

Enquiries to readers@constablerobinson.com.

Constable and Robinson Ltd (directly or via its agents)
may mail, email or phone you about promotions or products.

☐ Tick box if you do not want these from us ☐ or our subsidiaries.

www.right-way.co.uk
www.constablerobinson.com